THE ART OF FAKING IT

**SOUNDING SMART WITHOUT REALLY
KNOWING ANYTHING**

LAURENCE WHITTED-FRY

RUNNING PRESS
PHILADELPHIA · LONDON

9   8   7   6   5   4   3   2   1

Digit on the right indicates the number of this printing

Library of Congress Control Number: 2008928235

ISBN 978-0-7624-3297-4

Cover by Jessica Hische

Interior illustrations by Marc Rosenthal

Designed by Josh McDonnell

Edited by Jennifer Leczkowski

Special Thanks to Erin Slonaker

Typography: Archer, Cushing, and Helvetica

Running Press Book Publishers

2300 Chestnut Street

Philadelphia, PA 19103-4371

Visit us on the web!

www.runningpress.com

CONTENTS

ACKNOWLEDGMENTS

The author would like to thank, first of all, Michael Ross, a veritable fount of eternal cleverness, good spirits, and wisdom. And then, the cool and knowledgable Tara Callahan, Elizabeth Gold, Barbara Bayer, Victor Lederer, and Ben Finane.

Last and nowhere near least, mille grazie, vielen danke, muchas gracias, and merçi beaucoup to the remarkable Constance Sayre, who actually knows everything (except directions) and has the energy and generosity to share.

INTRODUCTION

Welcome to the Age of UnEnlightenment. Who today has time to be casually conversant about hip-hop culture, the newest breakthrough in computer technology, and/or the baby geniuses of independent cinema? No one. Yet just imagine how great it would feel if you could chat knowingly about Libeskind and Gehry or the tiny but charming vineyard in France where they're bottling a truly magnificent Musigny that almost no one can afford but everyone wants to drink!

The solution?

- Five years of grad school?
- A live-in tutor or "life-stylist"?
- Eight thousand dollars worth of reference books?

Not at all.

In this post-postmodern age, it is easier than ever to fake it: even real authorities are being challenged ("Well I guess scientists are entitled to their opinions"), Jon Stewart's fake news is more respected than the "real" news, and Ann Coulter is taken seriously. You, therefore, *can* be the ultimate authority.

What you're looking for is information—not all the information—just enough to overwhelm the people with whom you are speaking so that they acknowledge your superior sense of, well, everything. No one need know precisely which end of the double-wide was your room; now you can sound as if you're from, or spent childhood summers in, New York, Paris, Gstaad, the Hamptons, or any combination of these places instead of a small town in a state that begins and ends in a vowel. You have to learn to fake it, and we will supply the wherewithal. The best of information when hesitantly conveyed is received with skepticism—how you display your facts is as important as the facts themselves. In real estate it's location, location, location; in faking it it's attitude, attitude, attitude. It is important therefore for you to improvise your own repertoire of appropriate smiles, frowns, shrugs, and sneers while you offer the information you find in this book. Chances are you'll need to practice. Be diligent. While dressing in the morning, while logging on to the unemployment office, or while spinning or aerobicizing at the gym . . . keep practicing.

Once your style of delivery is perfected, all that remains is to commit this book to memory and steer any conversation toward one of your areas of expertise. Which will be many.

CHAPTER ONE

DRINKING

BOOZE, SPIRITS, COCKTAILS—
HOW TO ORDER THE RIGHT STUFF

Gone are the days when you could walk into a bar and simply order a vodka and tonic or a bourbon on the rocks. Brand names are part and parcel of the performance and ritual, and the most improbably lengthy conversations now take place about, Lord help us, designer vodka. And you certainly don't want to get caught with your snifter around your ankles, or whatever that expression is. So listen and learn.

VODKA

All vodka still smells vaguely like something used to sterilize a wound, if you can notice the smell at all, but its smell is its least important aspect. As liquors go, vodka is boring. One can describe a scotch or wine as being "mellow," "fierce," or any number of things, but you have

to fill vodka with essence of cranberry in order to give it any character. The first important thing to mention, often and loudly, is that all domestic vodkas taste the same. This is true, and spare us any conversation about the fact that Smirnoff was found, in a blind taste test, to be "the best." It isn't for you. It's too easy to find and much too cheap. Keep the conversation to eighty-proof vodkas, since the higher-proof ones can make you crazy anyway and are not for nice people.

The truly chic vodkas have kept to tradition and have no taste; this was presumably so that the drinker had no idea what he was doing while getting blasted, and it remains one of vodka's finest traits to this day. Clearly the trend toward infused vodkas, whether lemon, lime, hot pepper, currant, vanilla, or venison, is not for a respectable palate—it is for those who want to ingest every food group at cocktail time. Or, they're for grown-up kids who long for the days of Shirley Temples.

Stolichnaya, though still a fine vodka, is very "last millennium"; while once amazingly hip, Finlandia and Absolut are your father's vodkas. Ketel One, from Holland, utterly devoid of taste, is "in"; Grey Goose, an altogether unexciting quaff, has been marketed so well that the rich folk who are willing to spend double what other vodkas cost actually think it has a taste. Luksusowa, a Polish potato vodka that tastes oddly like gasoline and somehow manages to make people drunker faster, can be enjoyed with some freshly ground pepper on top. The heartburn factor here is very high, but it dazzles people. But for heaven's sake, have some self-respect and don't drink Trump vodka, the alcohol equivalent of a comb-over. There ought, by the way, to be a law against putting orange juice or other colorful liquids in these vodkas, so don't become part of a crime statistic. Good vodka should be drunk from the freezer or on the rocks with or without a twist of citrus; vodka martinis are still acceptable if there's no actual vermouth in the glass.

Sex and the City notwithstanding, avoid Cosmopolitans: they are anything but.

SCOTCH

The subject of scotches is far simpler. Scotch is rarely sullied the way vodka is, so "how to order" is not as much of an issue. If you prefer your scotch with ginger ale or cola, please move on to the next chapter. If not, pay heed.

For years, drinking Scotch whisky neat, i.e., without anything in it, was the only way. Researchers at the Drinkological Institute at Leaphroigh-upon-Nutting have, however, recently debunked that old wives' tale. Current wisdom has it that a splash of ice water (or add an ice cube or two and wait) releases some yummy chemicals and brings out whatever it is that's supposed to be brought out, flavor-wise. Unblended Scotches (aka Single Malt) still reign supreme; stick with the Highland or Islay regions. The Highland Scotches are sweeter and more honeyed, and the Islay Scotch is more peaty and smoky. The Macallan is the Highland Scotch to order—the eighteen-year-old is glorious, but the twenty-five-year-old is better, though unfortunately the latter is almost beyond financial reach. If, however, you're looking for peat and smoke—and who isn't?—Lagavulin is the Scotch for you. Though there's still nothing wrong with the snob-appealing, dense, malty scotches such as Laphroaig, Glenlivet, and Glenfiddich, you can one-up your tablemates (or barmates) who have ordered one of them with the epic pretension that comes with a little bit of knowledge. Those folks think they've got "taste," but a simple "Lagavulin, one ice cube," from you will put an end to the question of who's schooling whom.

BOURBON

Both Bourbon and Scotch are whiskeys. The difference is that Scotch is brewed in Scotland (no kidding) making Bourbon, essentially, America's scotch (note the lower case "s"). Well, the real stuff is very fancy and very strong: Booker's is the most ferocious. It's aged six years and nine months—a nice, if amazingly weird fact—and is 124.7 proof. It tastes of caramel and tobacco. Baker's is a mere 107 proof. Michter's ten-year tastes like butterscotch. These are small-batch bourbons—clearly not meant for just anybody. And then there's Jack Daniel's (just say "JD"). It is the only thing rednecks and advertising account executives have in common, and it should be treasured as such. You will, of course, just say that you know that Jack Daniel's isn't really bourbon—it has something to do with the way it's distilled and is none of your business unless moonshining is your hobby. You drink it neat, and if you're really looking to impress a redneck, a beer chaser will do. It's nauseating, you'll fall down drunk—it's hardly elegant—but it will shut up the people sitting in the Texas-like boozery in which you've accidentally found yourself. And it will make the account executives really sit up and play with their Blackberries, Treos, or whatever.

RUM

If you're in the sun and you must drink rum, try Cachaça, from Brazil. Mix it with fruit or fruit juice—lots of lemon and lime. (If you are thinking "cola," please stop thinking.) You may hallucinate, but it's a small price to pay for anything this esoteric. There is something called 151 rum—the stuff is 151 proof, which we didn't know was possible—but it won't get you the caché you're after unless your crowd is made up of pirates. And don't forget about Mojitos, the new Margaritas: they're cute, sweet, and tart enough to seem eccentrically acceptable. And they're green—very eco-sensitive.

TEQUILA

The mention of Margaritas brings us to Tequila. When people say, "Oh, I can't drink Tequila, it once made me so sick," they are no doubt referring to a night of debauchery that included either too many shots of Jose Cuervo or too many pitchers of sugar-filled Margaritas. Both should be avoided unless you are the type who still enjoys spring break or are appearing in *Girls Gone Wild #272—Staten Island*. "The secret to drinking Tequila," you must reply to your poor uninformed friend, "is to drink the good stuff, straight, and with lots of water backs."

Sadly, Cuervo has not constituted "the good stuff" since 1989. Fortunately, high-quality tequilas like Patrón have become relatively available, even in the boonies. In a pinch, Don Julio, Herradura, or even, strangely enough Sammy Hagar's Cabo Wabo (yes, Van Halen's Sammy Hagar) will do. Should you run across someone who is already drinking Patrón, you can always one-up them by declaring that Patrón is alright when Lapis is unavailable. If you want to impress and amuse even the most jaded bartender, order your Patrón "straight-up, no fruit, no vegetables, no training wheels, and not chilled." Don't forget the water back—one glass per shot. Follow these rules, and you can drink as much Tequila as you like. You may get drunk, and wake up with a hangover and/or a new "friend," but unlike with the cheap or sugary stuff, you will not long for the sweet release of death the next morning. If you must drink Margaritas, please have them made individually and with fresh limes. As for frozen margaritas—if you want a Slurpee, go to a 7-Eleven.

WINE

The Talking

In Vino Duplicitus . . .For many, wine is an intimidating subject, perhaps because there is among oenophiles that smug insiderness that can make one cringe, feeling like a child listening to the grown-ups talk. Also, there is the ridiculous descriptive vocabulary they use—starting with the word *oenophile*—and continuing into a multiplicity of strange appellations for wines, vintages, and types of grapes. It doesn't have to be this way, though. The wino (a much preferable term for one who loves wine) terminology is easily faked, and the pleasure is all about drinking the stuff, but the next-best pleasure is faking intimate knowledge of the great and near-great wines.

Youngish collectors slavishly follow one or more of the half-dozen or so published wine critics, buying the wines the gurus recommend. Collectors like bragging, and they might say, "I just bought ten cases of the '05 Screaming Eagle Cab—Parker rated it 99, and I'm saving it!" Does this mean that they bought it and have no plans to drink it?

The Parker in question is Robert Parker—not the author of the Spenser detective novels, but the world's most famous and influential wine writer. Craving the kind of financial rewards brought by a good review from Big Bob, many vintners have shifted their winemaking style to garner a high score in his famous newsletter, *The Wine Advocate*. He is so promiscuous with scores in the high 90s and even 100 that it seems inevitable he will eventually have to grant inflationary scores of 150—sort of the wine equivalent of Nigel Tufnel's comment about his guitar amp in *This Is Spinal Tap*: "It goes to eleven." Still you won't go too far wrong if you heed the qualities Parker likes and liberally employ the buzzwords he uses, such as:

Fruity, when used with regard to wine, is not an unenlightened pejorative having to do with a particular "lifestyle." It is, rather, one of the more obvious vino attributes—the stuff tastes like fruit. This is quickly replaced by coded, more "perceptive" characterizations as to the kind of fruitiness the wine under discussion expresses. A "fruit bomb" is a wine loaded with upfront tastes of fruit. This is the first stage of fruitiness, the next being "jammy," meaning pretty much the same thing, though this suggests cooked fruit. (If you find these terms a bit silly, just wait.) The final stage of this sequence is "port-like," which compares the wine under discussion to port, the fortified wine of Portugal. Port is thick in texture, sweet, and higher in alcohol than regular wine. Fruit flavor is not a bad thing if it is balanced by other qualities; if it is not, you might as well be drinking Hawaiian Punch.

Head-spinning alcohol content is a Parker-ism that moves the terminology into the land of the bizarre when you realize that he means it as praise, leading one to wonder: if you want to get blasted, why not just take a couple of healthy pulls straight from the vodka bottle? Or, if you must drink wine, why spend $40 for a French vintage when a couple of pints of Night Train would do the trick?

Gobs of toasty oak is not as weird as it sounds, since wines aged in oak barrels have a distinctive taste and smell that resemble vanilla, toast, or crème brulée—all tasty edibles. Overdone, it makes the wine smell like a lumberyard.

Tannic is not to be confused with tantric, which is a whole other issue, apparently involving sex with Sting. Tannin is a part of all wine's content to one degree or another. The term tannic is sometimes embellished by a bewildering range of modifiers, including sweet, dusty, soft, supple, chewy, ripe, firm, rough, harsh, astringent, palate-clenching, mouth-wringing, butt-puckering (okay we made that last one up—but only the last one). The stuff that evokes all this verbal groping is a chemical compound in grape skins and stems. Tannins give good, traditionally made red wines a dry, grippy feeling in the mouth; over the course of years they melt imperceptibly away into the wine. The true oenophile is unafraid of tannic wine, but if your palate is more used to Diet Dr. Pepper, just grin and bear it.

Finish refers not to wines from Finland but to what the rest of us call an aftertaste. It tells of a wine's concentration. Parker often describes wine's finish by length—starting at around 40 seconds and extending from there—as though he checks against a stopwatch. But for the newbie, "finish" is perhaps the easiest and earliest wino word to use, and will make you sound pleasantly up-to-speed.

Nose is another easy wine word; it means nothing more than smell. But how much more sophisticated to say "marvelous nose" than "smells awesome!"

Transparency is a noble ideal in which a wine's qualities are in harmony, with every element in place and clearly perceptible. Not to be confused with "tasteless."

And Then There's the Actual Wine (Finally!)

Become a Burgundy lover, the absolute ultimate in high-priced wine snobbery. Collecting Burgundy is trophy-hunting in its purest form, and there is plenty of label fondling going on. These wines include those of Bordeaux, and the Barolos and Barbarescos of the Piedmont in northwestern Italy. Meursault, a white Burgundy, nearly always evokes hazelnuts; reasonable since those of us not allergic have downed the occasional hazelnut and have a clear impression of its flavor. Comparisons with the citrus family are often legit as well; Meursault also may remind tasters of lime. Many great whites are called "steely"—you may be forgiven for being uncertain about the appeal of something that tastes like a carving knife.

Descriptions take on a decided air of fantasy when aficionados talk about hints of gooseberries and mulberries, the latter consumed only by silkworms. The rose petals and truffles beloved of Barolo drinkers are almost reasonable descriptions, but referring to a flavor being tinged with tar can unfortunately bring to mind the image of being on one's knees licking the pavement on a brutally hot day.

With Burgundy, made from the pinot noir grape, the rapturous ravings get truly insane. You should have little trouble keeping a straight face if you stick to describing young red Burgundy as smelling and tasting like strawberries, raspberries, cherries, and occasionally violets. More problematic is if the wine has an element of under-ripeness, usually (but not always) to the wine's detriment; you may then have to use terms such as vegetal, green, stemmy, or stalky. As Burgundy ages, though, the descriptors broaden out to include chestnuts, orange, and (ugh) tobacco. It typically evolves further toward licorice (a good sign), mushrooms, sous-bois (undergrowth, as in the woodland), resin, wet earth (yummy), coffee, toffee, and cocoa.

If you are beginning to think that, when describing wine, you can get away with saying almost anything that pops into your head, drunk or sober, you are not far off; especially when dealing with old red Burgundy. This drink takes on funky qualities that do not appeal to everyone but are heavenly to the hard-core fan. So to truly impress, you might have to describe them in terms of leather, smoked meat, "wet dog fur" (we kid you not), prunes, quince, and quinine (tonic water). The words "old sneakers and sweat socks" have been bandied about seriously, if rarely written down.

Some snobs drink nothing but the grand cru vineyards (the best growths of a region, and literally, "great growth") at the top of the hierarchy, which rarely cost less than $100 a bottle, nice work if you can get it—or fake it. Feel free to claim that your palate is too refined to drink the earthier wines from Nuits St. Georges or from the southern half of the growing region (the Côte de Beaune). Always refer to the wine from the vineyard Musigny as "Moose." Would that we were making this up! And naturally, you buy your Moose online, because if available at all in shops, it has been stored too long and incorrectly (and hanging out with lesser wines—horrors!).

Oh yes, wines in which the alcohol dominates disagreeably are called "hot," and almost all wines benefit from being allowed to "breathe," aerate, or oxygenate after the bottle is opened. Drinking it straight from the bottle is a no-no and does not count as helping it breathe through artificial respiration.

There you have it. You are now ready to go forth to your next restaurant gathering or dinner party and pontificate that the wine of the evening has, "An obnoxious little nose, with a taste of spinach, and some excrement in the finish."

CHAPTER TWO

EATING

COOKING, GIVING ORDERS, STAYING HEALTHY—STUFFING YOUR FACE WITH ÉLAN

COOKING

Each of us secretly considers him- or herself a good cook and a better eater, with wonderfully varied tastes. We shrug modestly while admitting that our Tripe à la Valenciana is world-revered and invite our host and hostess wholeheartedly "some time" for our veal with shiitakes in a lemon-lime reduction, all the while praising to the skies what we are eating at the moment. The problem is how to keep the conversation in your court or kitchen, so to speak. This way you can sound like a real expert, even if chicken wings and frozen pizza are really your favorite things to cook and eat. If it's ever possible to be esoteric and simple at the same time, this is it. There are, first of all, things not to do.

Do not:

- Brag about your quiche (this has-been has become as commonplace as cold breakfast cereal).
- Serve "pigs-in-blankets" at stand-up cocktail parties, unless ironically.
- Prefer restaurants with salad bars (in fact, you'd be wise to have never heard of one).
- Even acknowledge the existence of iceberg lettuce.
- Mention coq au vin or boeuf bourguignon in a discussion of French food (these dishes were okay thirty years ago but now are in the same category as quiche).
- Make a face or throw up at the mention of escargots (while they are no longer considered exotic—so liking them won't get you points—being appalled by them is gauche and will give you away instantly).
- Put ketchup on lamb.
- Prefer all your Italian food with red sauce.
- Salt your food before you taste it.
- Ask for a side order of fries or MSG.

Now that those are out of the way, here are some pieces of knowledge, bluffs, and attitudes to make you sound like a mini Julia Child or Wolfgang Puck.

- When you are served your salad with a fancy dressing, announce your preference for "the perfect vinaigrette," which only you and a few restauranteurs in the south of France know how to make. It consists of (you are graciously willing to share the secret) extra-virgin Spanish (not Italian, as everyone else thinks) olive oil, expensive vinegar (if Balsamic, a thirty-dollar-a-bottle brand and make sure to tell your listeners not to overdo it, but suggest rice wine vinegar is even more "special") and a dab of Dijon or other French mustard. Period.

- Say something like, "Coriander is the most misunderstood of spices."

- If anchovies make you sick (which is only right), say you don't like them because they bury the taste of everything they're served with—"one has to be so careful with them."

- State you newfound preference for American caviar. It's very chic and much cheaper than Caspian, which is currently banned for political reasons (apparently the fish have been seen in the company of suspected evildoers). The Seattle Caviar Company sells a golden, crunchy roe from Montana's Flathead Lake; four ounces for under $30.00. Delicious esoterica.

- Praise small, undecorated Chinese restaurants that are cheap.

- Undercook all vegetables.

- Serve pepper and salt from a dish or a mill, not a shaker.

- Only want Mexican or Indian food occasionally. The former "deadens the palate"; the latter "is never prepared properly in this country—they simply can't seem to get the right spices here."

- Regardless of what you're being served, ask your tablemates if they've ever tried adding a touch of vinegar to it while it's cooking. It always sounds like a good idea.

- If you must serve dessert, opt for fruit and cheese (Humboldt Fog or Prima Donna will do) instead of butterscotch ice cream with chocolate syrup.

- Of course, you will never cook for anyone, mostly because you're waiting for your new cookware from France, along with it the imported tarragon in sealed tubes. And if you truly never want to talk about cooking, plead total ignorance and explain how the family cook never allowed the family in "her" kitchen when you were a child.

HEALTH FOOD—
GETTING IN WITH THE MUNG BEAN AND SOY SET

The question that immediately springs to mind is "Why bother?" Health food addicts are a notoriously humorless, if purportedly healthy, lot. But if you have ever been in their company, the lone degenerate among these paragons of clean living, you know the answer. These energetic bundles of unsullied protein have a knack for making you feel like something that crawled out from under a rock. While normally content as an unrepentant Oreo lover, when placed among bran worshippers all your resolve seems to dissolve in a puddle of self-doubt. To help you through these times of trouble, here are some tips and catchphrases.

Mea Culpa. The basic rule of thumb: If it tastes good, it is bad for you. Similarly: The worse it tastes, the better it is for you. Twinkies, taco chips, even toast ("burns out the vitamins") are no-nos. You claim to snack on raw carrots and vile concoctions such as brewer's yeast and wheat germ oil mixed with goat's milk. Meat in general is out—"It makes you mean, man" and interferes with your mellowness. Organically fed chickens are a possibility (try to avoid cracks about them being fed brown rice and bean sprouts; it is probably true and, therefore, not funny). Professing pure vegetarianism for either human-itarian or health reasons is best, but if you must confess to eating "foods with a face," claim that you stick to fish and avoid red meat. This would seem to make fast-food burgers okay, since that meat (if it is meat) is probably far from red when it is finally cooked, but this is not the case.

If it makes you feel good, it is bad for you. No caffeine, nicotine, or alcohol allowed. You may be amazed at how many health-food freaks smoke, but keep in mind that one is not allowed to justify the act on the grounds that cigarettes are "vegetable matter."

Haute Cuisine: Forget it! The epitome of culinary art in the world of health food is the spinach salad. Anything else is too oily (bad for the skin), too rich (bad for the arteries), too spicy (bad for the stomach), or causes cancer. Creative cooking becomes difficult when the most exotic spice permitted is lemon juice. You may be assured of adulation from your "peers" by knowing twenty-five ways to prepare alfalfa sprouts (*avec sauce chocolate* is not allowed); you'll score extra points for growing your own in a hydroponic tank in the basement.

Vitamins A–Z. A shortcut or short circuit, if you will, to any conversation about vitamins is to maintain, "I never take vitamin capsules, I get all I need naturally in my diet" and "Between brown rice and mung beans, I get them all." Since one person's vitamin needs can be completely different from another's, almost any diet can be justified if pronounced confidently as "right for your system." "I live on bananas and bee pollen," said with just the right flair will sail you through any grilling on vitamin supplements.

Fasting. Not to be confused with dieting, one fasts not to lose weight but to "cleanse the system of impurities." Fasting can be used to gracefully get you out of eating proffered carrot-squash-and-soybean casserole when what you really want is a chunk of cheesecake. "I'm on a water fast" is a phrase guaranteed to set little health-food hearts aflutter and put the kibosh on any doubts as to your credentials.

Liquids. Tap water is taboo, and Perrier is for parvenus. True health-food fanatics drink only water from mountain streams above 13,000 feet or acidophilus shakes (about which the less said the better). An office-sized water cooler in your home is considered adequate proof of your earnestness. Juices are acceptable, fruit or vegetable, but must be squeezed in your own juicer. Do not run out and buy one, however, because cleaning it is one of the labors of Hercules. If you are forced to entertain a devotee of the whole-grain life, buy a small quantity of freshly made juice at the local health-food store and serve it as your own, ranting all the while about "how quickly the vitamins are lost."

Health-food restaurants are the pits. If possible steer the crowd to a Japanese restaurant. Japanese food is acceptable and differs from health food in that it is edible. If you are forced to go to a health-food restaurant, eat a steak before you leave the house—then you can order a bowl of miso soup and a grape and wow the assemblage with your "Eastern asceticism."

Faking one's way through the world of health foods is not all that difficult, because there is a certain amount of fakery already going on among the citizenry. A quick tour through any health-food store will reveal that attempts are being made to take the pain out of being healthy. You will spy health-food candy that would turn Mars & Co. green with envy.

Health-food types are at least subliminally aware that all is not right, and even the most hardened brown-rice junkie will occasionally down an entire box of chocolate donuts in a nervous fit. This thread of guilty secrets runs through all advocates of the Whole Foods Way, which is why you have an advantage. As a guiltless devourer of chemicals, insecticides, and carcinogens, you have the upper hand in this game of one-upmanship. You can pontificate confidently on the joys of goats' milk yogurt, secure in the knowledge that you will never go near the stuff. Your attendants, on the other hand, will fear to press you on the issue lest you reveal that only last week you saw them furtively washing down hot dogs with beer!

SUSHI—RAW, RAWER, RAWEST

Friends, you're either with the sushi lovers and liked, or you're against them and looked down upon. Sushi consumption plays a pivotal role in modern-day American society. What was once considered an eccentric and foreign quirk is now considered a hip and necessary affectation, especially among white urbanites who favor black clothing, but it's happening all over. Granted, redneck sushi is spicy chicken wings wrapped in wasabi'd Uncle Ben's, but it's ubiquitous.

In order to fake that you like sushi and appear as if you consume aquatic vertebrates other than frozen fish sticks and their invertebrate and unidentifiable tater tot counterparts, you must first learn a few tidbits of information that you can drop during the dining experience.

How's this? A report in an online issue of the *Journal of Neuroscience* indicates that a diet rich in omega-3 fatty acids may ward off Alzheimer's disease. Those omega-3s are rampant in sushi. This is at once entertaining and interesting, and it will help you look as if you read newspapers, *Newsweek*, and important medical journals, let alone the *Journal of Neuroscience*. Occasionally browse the Internet for fascinating sushi facts to share with your dining companions. What you will not mention are tales of disturbing parasites, as these will only make you seem mortal and plebian. And whatever you do, don't joke about how this stuff would be fine if they just cooked it a little.

It is always impressive when someone knows just what to order at the sushi bar, so before exiting your house, Google the word *sushi* and jot down a few key "must have" phrases onto a small business card so you can run to the restroom and read it before the actual ordering begins. There are plenty of sushi snobs on the Internet willing to tell you just what to pick and choose to make you Asiatically likable. Here are some terms to get you started:

- **Nigiri**
The typical sushi consisting of an oblong mound of sushi rice with a speck of wasabi and a slice of fish. Possibly bound with a thin band of nori (seaweed), and is often served in pairs. Be prepared for the occasional wasabi overdose if the chef went heavy on the mustard. In this event try to disguise your tears, or failing that, say how you are moved by the beauty of the food's presentation (very Japanese).

- **Maki**
This is the rolled sushi, usually cut into six or eight pieces, which constitutes an order. These can also include cucumber, thinly sliced carrots, or avocado. Sushi is a protein festival, and this is as close as you are likely to get to a green vegetable in a sushi place. Some rolls now include mayonnaise. And you thought it was gross before!

- **Ebi: Shrimp**
This is cooked shrimp, like a shrimp cocktail shrimp—as safe as you will get.

- **Ama-Ebi: Raw shrimp**
Good luck.

- **Fugu: Blowfish**
This is literally deadly if not properly prepared. Order only if being hip is more important than life itself.

- **Hamachi: Yellowtail Tuna**
Delicious but not daring.

- **Hamaguri: Clam**
Something you might already like.

- **Maguro: Tuna**
Very rich and very good but will win you no points.

- **Sashimi**
Essentially sushi without the rice (though a bowl may be served on the side). May seem like sushi-plus, but it is actually less elegant and so rich that you will be hard-pressed to finish a meal.

- **Unagi: Freshwater eel**
Sounds like a high *ick* factor but in fact is usually cooked with a tasty barbecue-like sauce. Not to be confused with . . .

- **Uni: Sea urchin roe**
Which looks like something cleared from a baby's diaper and tastes like the ocean floor.

It's always great to be able to relate personal stories while eating sushi, so even if you've never been to Japan, you can lie. Just make sure that your companions haven't been, either. Sushi eaters tend to be well-traveled, and it's important to appear part of the global community. Even if in your case that community starts with www. Most of the people you're trying to overwhelm won't know you well enough to realize you've never left the continent. So, again, go to the Internet and weave together believable personal tales about how you had the best eel in

Hamamatsu when you were twelve. If you're close to getting caught, remind them that, for heaven's sake, you were only twelve, and it was the same day you and your parents met the Emperor.

And lastly, if a friend invites you to a sushi place and you arrive only to notice that you are one of three couples gracing the establishment, immediately launch into a monologue about how one must never enter a sushi restaurant that one can get into without a bit of acrobatics and name dropping, especially since, if the place is half-empty, the sushi must be old, old, old. Then make up some sort of excuse utilizing your trusty cell phone, and leave. This will allow you to go home and eat your frozen fish sticks and tater tots in peace, while at the same time seeming terrifically discerning and omniscient about all things raw.

FAKING YOUR WAY INTO THE TRENDIEST RESTAURANTS—HOW TO GET A TABLE WHEN YOU DON'T HAVE A RESERVATION AND THE PLACE IS FULLY BOOKED

You're in L.A. or New York on business. Someone—or several people—who can do you a great deal of professional good want to go the hippest, newest restaurant du jour. You wish to impress them with your consummately cosmopolitan aplomb and power. The restaurateurs in question don't know you from a hole in the ground, but you're certainly not going to let your business associate know that. The restaurants have been booked a month in advance. You have until the following evening. What do you do? Panic? Never! You get into the restaurant. How? With *chutzpah.*

It is crucial to remember whom you are dealing with here. Like dogs and horses, restaurant reservation bookers respond to an authoritative voice, they like to be flattered, and they like to be grov-eled to—not necessarily in that order. All chef-owners know each other, too, so if you know one (or claim to), another will treat you like an hon-ored guest, especially if you explain that Chef A made you promise you would eat at Chef B's place when you were in Chef B's town.

Call the restaurant.

RESTAURANT: Good evening, may I help you?

YOU: Yes, my name is Smith and I'm calling to confirm my reserva-tion for tomorrow evening and change it from three to four people [or vice versa—any other change means a different size table and is rude to suggest, although fives and sixes can be switched as well].

RESTAURANT: (after a pause) I'm sorry, sir, we don't seem to have any reservation in that name.

YOU: (slightly perturbed) Well, that's not my fault, is it? I made the reservation myself almost a month ago, and I will only be here for another day. What do you suggest?

You are now past the "authoritative voice" stage. You have his ear, but he is not about to help you. You continue:

YOU: But I never go to another restaurant when I'm in [city]. I can still remember the perfect dinner I had a couple of weeks ago when I was with those five Japanese businessmen. They said it was the high point of their visit to the United States, and I'm certain it was.

You have now gotten to "flattery," and the suggestion that you spent hundreds of dollars on a recent meal at their establishment. He is beginning to perk up.

> **YOU:** (with a slight whine in your voice) Isn't there anything you can do for me? Check your reservations once again? Put me on a waiting list? Any hour tomorrow evening would be fine, even though I specifically made the reservation for eight o'clock.

You have now begun to grovel, all the while holding firm to your original statement—that you had a reservation to begin with. You will, in fact, be put on a waiting list and told to call back the following day—which you will obediently do, and often. If you should speak to another person the following day, explain to him or her that the person you spoke with (whose name you know by now) the day before had virtually promised you a table for that evening. And don't worry, you'll get in.

Another ploy involves calling, once again, to confirm, using a heavy South American or British accent and claiming you are the secretary to señor and señora Argento, or Lord and Lady Winston. When faced with the inevitable "There is no reservation," claim you called from your "native" land well over a month ago and state that you hope there hasn't been a mix-up. (This is stage 1—authoritative voice.) The meal at their restaurant means everything to your employers—they always eat there, often under other names, to avoid being recognized. They only eat the best, hence their frequent visits. (Stage 2—flattery.) If you still haven't been put on a waiting list or been confirmed, remember Stage 3—groveling. Explain that you will lose your job if the mix-up turns out to be your fault, and beg them to try really hard to accommodate your employers. You are a man of the people and so is the person who writes down the reservations—a nice touch. Follow the instructions earlier for the following day's calls.

The final attack is one that requires a bit of easy research. You must know the names of two chefs, cities apart. As we mentioned earlier, they all know and respect each other, and so it is your job to tell Chef A that Chef B had promised to make the reservation for you himself, and you simply can't believe he forgot. Trust us, what with making sauces out of partridge lungs, lime, foam, and feathers, they don't have time to call each other to confirm. Refer to Chef B by his first name. Authority, flattery, and just a touch of groveling again will do the trick.

CHAPTER THREE:

MAKING IT WITH WOMEN

THE MAN'S GUIDE TO THE (UN)FAIR SEX

The secret to faking it with women is understanding women. "Impossible," you say? True enough, but one secret to even vaguely comprehending women is the knowledge that while they are as different as snowflakes in most respects, in one way they are all alike— confused when it comes to men. One has only to watch a babe like Angelina Jolie, who could have her pick of any man in the world, go from Billy Bob Thornton to Brad Pitt; Christie Brinkley flit from French heirs and artists to, well, Billy Joel; or recall that Marilyn Monroe bedded a baseball player, a playwright, and most likely a president to know that this is veritas. Case closed. "No!" women cry, "we just have catholic tastes, unlike you men who stick to one type: endless permutations of your mother!" Not true (well, maybe there's a shred of something to the part about mothers). Women vacillate between such extremes because they are all secretly searching for the same type—a non-existent hybrid of James Bond and Jon Stewart.

In other words, the answer to "What do women want?" is "They don't know." On the one hand, they want someone who is safe, secure, modest, reliable, gentle, tender, and madly in love with them. On the other hand, they want a wild, impetuous, crazy, dangerous, roughneck romantic who "frankly doesn't give a damn"—and they want both to be the same person. "No one but a schizo could be both," men cry out, "and even he wouldn't be both at the same time!" True, but the good news is that every man contains the seeds of both a CPA and a biker despite the fact that he leans one way or the other most of the time. The secret to getting and holding a woman is to beef up the part that is not naturally your own personality, and to do this you must Fake It.

If you have the body of Beckham and Bill Gates's money, as well as a sense of humor and a Harley-Davidson 750 that you regularly ride on the handlebars at 100 mph, you probably have little trouble attracting women. Keeping them around is another story. Women may be confused, but any that you might want to keep are not stupid. They know that your type goes through them like six-packs of beer, and no smart girl wants to end up being the empty Buds, so they often drop you before you drop them.

Your job is to throw them off guard. Just when they have you pegged as a typical, macho, love-'em-and-leave-'em type, burst into tears. When asked what is wrong, you say, "It's nothing, just free-floating anxiety; it will pass." While they are reeling from that, tell them that you are really "terrified of the void," and that your macho personality is just your "existential way of dealing with it." By the time they figure out that you don't know what you are talking about (assuming they do), you will be home free. In art this is called "undercutting"—taking an obvious image and throwing a curve ball.

Another example would be taking off your leather pants (your type should have no problem reaching this stage) to reveal hand-monogrammed, custom-made, pure silk shorts. This upsets a woman's preconceived image of you. In addition, women find androgyny extremely attractive (see Johnny Depp).

As we have pointed out, wild and crazy types have less trouble getting women than holding on to them. When they start throwing your clothes out onto the street, it is your job to convince them that your philandering is your problem and is no threat to them. Try lines like "I only fool around because I'm afraid I might be gay" or "I know I'm not good enough for you." (Try to say these things before she does; they are definitely more effective that way.) Fail, and she will eventually dump you "for her own preservation"; succeed too well and actually settle down, and she will dump you out of boredom—"You're not as much fun as you used to be." The trick is to find the combination that keeps her.

Conversely, if you are the quiet, stable type, you have trouble attracting women in the first place, or else find that though you have a lot of women friends, you haven't had sex in five years. Your main problem is that you believe what women tell you: that they appreciate your sensitivity and warmth, and it is wonderful to be able to talk to you, "not like that crazy Jimmy or Frankie" (whom they only boink). They mean it—they do appreciate you—it's just that they take you for granted and find you about as sexually exciting as doing the laundry.

Well, it is easier than you think to change that. Try to hint about some trouble before you met them: "We were doing a job overseas . . . a man died . . . I can't really talk about it . . ." "If I had known that my father had been . . . oh never mind." Choke up, and finish with, "Let's not get into that now."

Start showing up late (or better still, not at all) for dates with girls who "just want to be friends," but whom you would like to ravish. Explain with, "Gee, I'm sorry, but I got into this thing with this gal at work," then immediately change the subject. No need to elaborate as to who the "gal" might be or what exactly the "thing" was—let her imagination do the work.

Best of all, get drunk—sloppy drunk—and make a fool out of yourself, or, even better, pick a fight (not with the girl, stupid) and be carried out of a bar—there is nothing like it for shocking platonic girlfriends out of their complacency. Once they begin to view you in this new light, it is a short trip to the bedroom with this former friend.

Once you are firmly ensconced as her lover and roommate, holding on is merely a matter of keeping her from getting bored and, once again, taking you for granted. Your naturally agreeable personality will keep her basically happy, but it doesn't hurt to occasionally stay out all night without calling. Be sure to come home with an incredibly flimsy excuse.

Women are actually easy to please. If you are Clive Owen, temper it with a little Jay Leno, if you are essentially Steve Carell, give them a little Nicolas Cage. It is not necessary to change your basic personality, just spice it up with some Dr. Jekyll or Mr. Hyde, whichever is needed. Remember, when Woody Allen gave Diane Keaton a little Bogey in *Play It Again, Sam,* she fell for it . . . and him!

CHAPTER FOUR:

MAKING IT WITH MEN

THE WOMAN'S SIDE

The phone has stopped ringing. It seems like you haven't had a date since the junior prom. Why, you wonder? Could it be that you started snoring when Ralph was explaining the workings of his fuel-injected Ferrari? Or maybe it was because you burst into hysterical laughter when John told you that he was having a lot of success with his all-broccoli and pineapple diet. "But I was just reacting honestly," you protest. This is fine if you enjoy the social life of a nun. But if you want the attentions of the male of the species, you will have to learn to Fake It.

It has become increasingly difficult to fake it with guys in order to make it with guys. Thanks to the proliferation of unconscionable lad magazines and insidious Internet sites that show the most perfectly airbrushed and beautiful people on the planet and portray them as the norm, it's hard to fake anything anymore. Unless you are outstandingly beautiful, at all times, in all lights, your chances of breaking a man are grim at best.

"The women in magazines never have a stray nipple hair," they say. Despite this trend, when looking to rein in a man there are some time-honored traditions that you can adhere to in order to further your Man Harnessing Cause. The first of these things should have been learned in the sandboxes of your youth.

1. Ignore them entirely.
Bar none, this is the fastest way to get a man interested in you. Indifference is pivotal to the mating ritual and stems back to the dawn of time. Regardless of what you were taught to believe by modern-day society or Gloria Steinem, there is an alpha and there is a beta in every relationship, and you best remember how to play beta, or else. Not *be* beta. *Play* beta. There is a difference. The simple act of knowing you are renders you not. Fake disinterest, ladies. Fake it with every single fiber of your being and then fake it three times more.

2. Find someone else.
Remember, we're part of an animal kingdom. What works for monkeys, ferrets, and whales will work for you. There is nothing more enticing to a man or a whale than the woman/whale fascinated by another. Pick the hottest, most attractive and successful man in your 'hood, and date him. Pay him if you need to.

3. Become bi-sexual.
Women by nature are beautiful. Two women attracted to each other are 500 times as beautiful. This stunt ups your odds 5000 percent. In the presence of a man, grab your best-looking pal, and touch her, not even intimately (unless you want to), but simply touch her in a way that insinuates intimate affection. A simple stroke to the face should suffice. Maybe something to do with lotion. Perhaps Coppertone. A beach.

Malibu. Then be prepared for a veritable onslaught of testosterone the likes of which you have never seen.

4. Play dumb.

I know this will make you want to slit your wrists and drown yourself in Vicodin/vodka cocktails, but you must. You are allowed to be witty. You are allowed to be funny. You are allowed to be charming.

But never, ever, EVER, while in your fake man-harnessing-bubble are you allowed to be more funny, more witty, or more charming than the man you are attempting to break. While you are expected to find even his oldest "knock-knock" jokes hilarious, you must never under any circumstances laugh at a man. Only about 25 percent of the male population has anything remotely resembling a sense of humor about themselves (in Europe, it is close to .000006 percent).

When he tells you his first wife left him because he "was too much 'man' for her," awed sighs are appropriate; guffaws are not. When the two long strands of hair that he is combing across his otherwise bald head are blown by the wind so that they hang below his chin, try to focus on something of interest on his belt buckle until he rearranges them. Holding your sides and turning red will not lead to expensive dinners and island getaways.

5. Learn to love sports.

Yes boooooring, but very important to men, so you might as well understand them. It is not necessary to actually watch the games, since everything of interest that happens will be rebroadcast on the evening news. This is because most of the game is taken up with things like time-outs, halftimes, huddles, conferences on the pitcher's mound, etc. You must never, of course, say this to a man—to him, every minute of a game is as important as finding the cure for cancer.

Forced to watch a game with a man? Feel free to read a book—he will be too absorbed in the game to notice. You need only look up during the commercials and when you hear the announcers going wild. They will then show an instant replay of whatever they were excited about, so you won't miss anything.

6. Ask about his (fascinating) work.

Remember too, a man "is" what he "does." He takes his work very seriously, and he loves to talk about it. If you are planning an evening with a CPA or an insurance salesman, drink a pot of coffee before he picks you up. Try to get him to take you to a movie or a concert—anywhere the opportunity for conversation is limited. A show of some kind will also give you a topic, other than his work, for discussion.

Do not expect to talk about your work —he will either assume that you are only doing it until Mister Right comes along, or, if you convince him that you are serious about your career, he will become instantly impotent. Which brings us to . . .

7. Get sexy.

A recent poll among males eighteen to sixty-five asked: True or False, "Men only want one thing." As you may have guessed, 98.2 percent answered true. Men are hypocrites about many things, but this is not one of them. They may lie to you, but rest assured they are not lying to themselves.

We are told that one-night stands are now okay for women. This is true if that is all you want from a guy. If, on the other hand, you meet a fellow who seems on the surface to be neither a creep, moron, momma's boy, nor a professional stud and you think you might want an ongoing relationship, hold out. Even if you want to tear his clothes off immediately—control yourself.

There is no need to put off sex until you are married, but if you hop into bed shortly after "hello," it definitely reduces your air of mystery. Besides, many a "dreamboat" on the first date has turned into a garbage scow by the third, and you may lament the loss of someone who doesn't rate your tears. This may be starting to sound like *The Rules* for young moderns, but it is true that for men the "grass is always greener." The longer you stay on the other side of the fence, the longer they will hang around. In anticipation of the deed, wear matching and sexy undergarments. Yes, yes, you have 65 pairs of cotton underpants and one matching pair of lacy lingerie. Invest. Pretend every single day of your Man Harnessing Life that you may be called upon by Calvin Klein to model exactly what you have on under that get-up. I don't care if lace gives you hives. Do it, ladies. Embrace lace.

Have long-flowing tresses. And here we are, from whence we came, in the animal kingdom. Grow or buy a mane. You can now pay someone else to sew additional and flowy human hair onto your head and pretend you're Lindsay Lohan. Pay a stylist. Get the long hair. Perhaps augment it with a Mystic Tan, as all extensions look better against a tawny background.

When at last you have consummated the relationship, he will ask, "How was it for you?" If you desire ever to see this man again, you must resist the urge to say things like, "How was what?" Say "the earth moved"—he won't laugh (see earlier). Say he "is the best." Everyone else has lied, and if you don't think so, it is your problem.

The truth of the matter is that no matter what they say, men do not want to hear the truth. Tell him, "That plaid jacket and striped pants combination is so distinctive—so you." Tell him, "Actuarial science has always been a secret fascination of mine." Tell him, "Virgo, what's yours?" and "That's alright, it happens to everyone."

8. Pretend to cook.

Sure, the last time you turned on your stove you nearly burned down the apartment complex because the oven instructions were still tucked inside waiting for you to read them. This does not matter. Pretend. Call a caterer. Discard the boxes, put the food in pots that you can borrow from your neighbor, and reheat. Reheating is almost cooking, so when your man tells you what a great cook you are and you thank him, it will be coming from the land of white lies and not a fiery and punishing hell of deceit.

Do all of these things, and you too will find your soul mate . . . or at the very least a bipedal primate. Sometimes that's the best you can hope for.

If you don't have the stomach for it—well, there's always the convent.

CHAPTER FIVE

CLASSICAL MUSIC

EMPHASIS ON "CLASS"

Flat statements are the order of the day here. They imply vast knowledge. Herewith:

- Ludwig von Beethoven's symphonies are a numbers game: 3, 5, 7, and 9 are the best. The sixth is also fine; 1, 2, and 4 are not as inspired, and 8 is "like boot camp for 9."

- Of LVB's five piano concertos (*concerti* is correct, but it is a bit much), the fifth is the most famous and popular. You prefer the fourth. It is greater.

- Ravel's *Boléro* and Tchaikovsky's 1812 *Overture* are both stupid pieces, Bo Derek and cannons notwithstanding. You don't listen to Tchaikovsky. He is for children and the ballet.

- Mozart was perfect and the play/film *Amadeus* slandered him, although he did like to gamble. He composed forty-one symphonies, twenty-seven piano concertos, lots of operas, and hundreds of other works. Everything he wrote after the age of puberty is worth listening to.

- Handel's *Messiah* is great despite its popularity. You prefer it performed as it is written, with a small orchestra and chorus. Modern arrangements make it sound like a small war. *Messiah* sing-alongs are as hideous as karaoke.

- Johann Sebastian Bach was a humble, religious, hardworking man but apparently had time to create twenty-one children. All of his sons who lived became composers, the best of whom was Carl Philipe Emanuel Bach. You like all of J. S. Bach's music and once you "finally came to terms with" the suites for solo cello, you realized they were, like his *St. Matthew Passion*, among the pillars of Western music.

- Schubert's *Unfinished Symphony* (the eighth) is as finished as he wanted it to be. He died young, like Mozart, but unlike Mozart, of syphilis.

- Haydn is the greatest, but he's "so perfect he's almost dull, but to listen carefully is to understand his humor." He wrote—count 'em—104 symphonies, the last twelve of which are the most famous, but his "Paris" symphonies are "the most pungent." His string quartets are "paradigmatic."

- You are sick of Brahms and have no patience for Bruckner. You loved Mahler from the start—even the wrist-slashing sixth and the "intolerably sad but sublime" ninth, and you appreciate him more every time you listen.

- Most contemporary orchestral music is impossible to listen to. Those guys just write for other musicians, not the public.

- Some Stravinsky is great, e.g., *The Symphony of Psalms*. His ballet, *Le Sacre du Printemps* caused a riot in Paris in 1910, when music still mattered. His music is "too angular," though his "neo-Classical" phase remains fascinating in its innovations.

- You love thirteenth- to fifteenth-century music scored for choir and brass that was written to be performed in churches in Venice. It is "joyful, yet solemn." Hildegard von Bingen, the twelfth-century nun, was a great mystic and her music is "ethereal."

- You love the Chicago Symphony and Cleveland Orchestra. You do not like the Boston Pops—and what is "The Hollywood Bowl"?

Allow others to talk and then change the subject to one of the above. Speak enthusiastically and with the right combination of reverence and verve.

THE WORLD OF OPERA

Opera used to be blissfully easy to ignore, but since the invention of the late Beverly Sills and Luciano Pavarotti, it has become an issue. The Public Broadcasting System has added to the problem. With a flick of the wrist one can turn the TV dial from the relative safety of Oprah (not to be confused with "opera"), *The Sopranos* (*not* to be confused with sopranos), MTV, and *Everyone Used to Love Raymond* and find all manner and combination of tenors, sopranos, and baritones on a stage. Some are in lavish costumes, some are in evening clothes standing in front of an orchestra. And now there are operas coming to a movie theater near you. Everyone is singing in a foreign language, all are radiating the desire to be understood. Of course, they cannot be, and that is why the subtitle was invented—for the poor few of us who do not speak Italian, French, and German.

It is sad, but opera has become so accessible that it is getting harder and harder to admit that you know nothing about it. And so this primer for the ill-informed is designed to help you keep your head at least above water with a real aficionado (who won't let you talk much, anyway) and to dazzle the millions of people who think that opera was created by the rich, for the rich. They, by the way, are right.

General Information:
- Italian opera has beautiful melodies.
- German opera is long and "heavy."
- French opera has ballets and choruses.
- Russian opera is *Boris Godunov.*
- British opera is by Benjamin Britten, is in English, and the words are indecipherable.
- American opera is actually becoming a viable possibility; many are

performed but few of them last. John Adams, Philip Glass, and
William Bolcom are three active American opera composers.

A WORD OR TWO ABOUT MOZART

- He wrote his first opera when he was twelve. It is called *La Finta
  Semplice*, is short and uninteresting, "but isn't it interesting that a
  twelve-year-old could write an opera?"
- *Don Giovanni* is the greatest opera ever written, but *The Magic
  Flute* (referred to only as Flute by Those In The Know) has the most
  glorious music.
- *The Marriage of Figaro* is delightful, and it is okay to approve of it
  in English. This is because "so much of the wonderful humor is lost
  in Italian." This is the only opera you may not prefer in the original
  language.

WAGNER AND HIS PROBLEMS

- He was a rotten human being.
- He married Franz Liszt's daughter, and he cheated on her.
- He wrote the words and the music to his operas.
- *The Ring* cycle is sixteen hours long and is too much for you. But
  you love *Tristan and Isolde*. It has sensual music. The opening chord
  of the opera wanders around in trouble until the opera's final
  moment, more than four hours later.
- He was Hitler's favorite composer (see "rotten human being").

VERDI AND PUCCINI

- Verdi is greater, but Puccini is "moving and realistic."
- Verdi wrote in three basic periods—early, middle, and late. (We're not kidding; this is real opera terminology.)
- Verdi wrote *Otello* when he was seventy-three, *Falstaff* when he was seventy-nine. They are up there with *Don Giovanni* for greatness.
- Puccini died before he finished *Turandot*, and it was completed by Franco Alfano, who also wrote an opera called *Cyrano de Bergerac* which almost no one cares about.
- Puccini's *Madama Butterfly* has the saddest heroine in opera; *La bohème* has the most realistic characters. His opera *La fanciulla del west* takes place in Sacramento, California." (No, we're not inventing this.)

OTHER COMPOSERS—A ROUNDUP

- Rossini (*The Barber of Seville, William Tell*) retired at thirty-seven and threw parties in Paris.
- Bellini died at thirty-four and wrote operas that are hard to sing.
- Donizetti contracted syphilis and wrote very little after he was thirty-five. He did, however, manage to squeeze in almost seventy operas.
- Mascagni never wrote anything as good as *Cavalleria Rusticana.*

This is enough knowledge for anyone. If you pass the following test, you are ready to buck even the most headstrong buff. Match the pairs.

Answers appear nowhere in this volume. Good luck!

1. Hansel   A. letto

2. La   B. Callas

3. Arturo   C. Traviata

4. Rigo   D. Gretel

5. Maria   E. Toscanini

Andrea Bocelli? Just say "NO."

CHAPTER SIX:

JAZZ

COOOL, MAN!

"Jazz came up from New Orleans, Louis Armstrong blah, blah, blah . . ." Trust us: only Ken Burns and Wynton Marsalis talk about jazz like that. As in most of modern life, opinions are more important than facts. It's just a matter of artfully sprinkling your conversation with a few choice tidbits.

You must remember that there are only two important types of jazz: mainstream and avant-garde. Jazz-rock or fusion, once derisively called fuzak, seems to be attempting a comeback, but we can only hope for a knockout in the first round. Mainstream jazz is any style in which all the musicians play in the same key and time signature; in avant-garde jazz such considerations take a poor second to being angry and intellectual, European, or ADD afflicted.

Depending on which camp you are addressing, feel free to use the following pontifications.

You are mainstream speaking to avant-garde. "That stuff doesn't communicate, it's musical masturbation" or less heavy-handedly, "That stuff may be fun to play, but it is impossible to listen to." (Do not preface sentences with *like*; no one who cares about jazz has talked that way since 1963. However, *man*, used judiciously, is still acceptable. Save dude for your conversations about rock, and then only with young people [see page 62].)

You are avant-garde speaking to mainstream. "That stuff is no longer relevant to the chaos of post-modern existence," or "Hasn't that ground already been sufficiently covered?"

If you don't want to stop the conversation quite that dead, you will need to know the following:

Unlike rock, there are or were few if any "bands" in jazz (Weather Report was a notable exception). Players group and regroup with the regularity of a suburban "swap" club, and you can't tell the players without a score card, so here is a list to help you pretend that you know who's who and "what's happenin'." The good news is that the legends, living and dead, will still stand you in good stead, as there hasn't been a new player of equal note since the seventies.

SAXOPHONE

John Coltrane: Trane—as you will always refer to him—is oddly God for both mainstream and avant-garde alike. You "love *Ascension*" (the album) but "can't listen to it very often" (most people can't listen to it at all); however, you feel *Ballads* is "secretly his best album."

You love Charlie Parker, Lester ("Prez") Young, Sonny "He hasn't had a band worthy of him in years" Rollins, and Wayne Shorter (with Miles Davis, not Weather Report). The recently deceased Michael Brecker and the un-deceased Joe Lovano will be the only more recent names you need. If you must, you can throw around more current names, like Steve Coleman and Greg Osby, and talk about the Brooklyn M-Base collective, but be aware that nobody really cares.

If you dig avant-garde, it's Albert Ayler, Eric Dolphy, and Ornette Coleman.

PIANO

McCoy Tyner, a former Coltrane sideman, you claim "has never made a bad album." Thelonius Monk was as holy as his name implies, and you love his "quirkiness and angularity." Chick Corea (not to be confused with North or South Korea) is "best as a composer," and you "liked his group Return to Forever, pre- and post-guitars." As for Keith Jarrett, either you admire his love of the piano as a solo acoustic instrument or you consider him to be "the biggest wanker" you have ever heard; there is no middle ground with Keith.

You love (mainstream) Bill Evans, Art Tatum, Herbie Hancock (pre- and post-fusion). Extra points for throwing around the names of more obscure talents like Herbie Nichols and some modern names like

Brad Mehldau and Cyrus Chestnut. For the classic avant, Cecil Taylor stands out; for more recent cred, toss out Matthew Shipp, Sylvie Courvoisier, and Bugge Wesseltoft (we are not making that up).

BASS

The late Charlie Mingus is the legend in residence, more as a composer and musical genius than as a technician. Ron Carter "hasn't done much since the Miles quintet days" (see Miles, below). Stanley Clarke "was great at nineteen, but he picked up an electric bass, and his taste went out the window." For mainstream, you love Eddie Gomez and Charlie Haden. More recently, John Patitucci has "gone from fleet-fingered fusion antics to more mainstream maturity." (If you want to sound like a true critic, you get extra points for alliteration whenever possible.)

For avant bass players, William Parker will suffice.

TRUMPET

Miles and Dizzy—Dizzy and Miles—they are all ye know and all ye need to know. Miles Davis (never actually use his full name, or the jig is up) made some of the greatest jazz albums ever recorded. You love *Kind of Blue* ("doesn't everybody?"), *Miles Smiles*, and *E.S.P.*, and, "yes, his seminal fusion album *Bitches Brew* was great, but God, what crimes have been committed in its name." Dizzy Gillespie, always "Dizzy" or "Diz," wrote the classic "Night in Tunisia" and is "technically phenomenal, the 'be-bop master.'" Don Cherry or Lester Bowie (not to be confused with David or Jim) will suffice for avant. Wynton Marsalis can play but is stuck in the past and you "wish he would shut up already."

DRUMS

At nineteen, in Miles's quintet, Tony Williams "took the drums some-where else"—refuse to specify where. Jack DeJohnette was a "black fire on the otherwise cold, white, ECM label of jazz chamber music." (He is not dead, he just isn't on ECM anymore.) You love Max Roach and Elvin Jones (former Trane sideman). Paul Motian sounds like "someone falling down the stairs, but in a good way." For more outside stuff, you can bandy about names like Tom Rainey and Han Bennink (you love his sense of humor).

GUITAR

If you wish to be a true mainstream jazz snob, you don't even consider the guitar a jazz instrument.

CHAPTER SEVEN:

POP AND ROCK

FAKING IT WAS NEVER EASIER

The thorough Balkanization of the music industry has made faking musical hipness easier than ever. In the ancient era of the eighties, it was still possible for the music fan to be at least vaguely aware of all the artists, bands, and personalities in the biz. Since the paradigm shifting oughts, no one can keep track of all the genres of rock and pop music, let alone all the players. Thus you need simply counter any hipster's references to the music he/she insists is cool with a terse dismissal and a reference to a distant sect that they know nothing about.

For example, confronted with a lover of obscure indie/college noise rock, you profess a penchant for ironic eighties pomp-rock bands who sound like Queen. Always remember: irony is your friend. Even if you slip, and mention your Barry Manilow collection, all you have to do—after the gasps of the fashionistas have subsided—is to say, "Well, of course I am into him ironically." Anything that begins in England is hipper than if it started in the USA, except the Ramones, who, you must insist, invented punk music. Hipper still are bands from the foreign country du jour (at this writing Canada is leading the pack—whoda thunk it?).

Should you be tempted to delve in more detail, be warned: the Wikipedia entry for a mere subgenre of Punk rock—"Emo"—lists no less than seventy-five bands in an effort to describe what Emo means. Apparently it refers to Punk rockers who, having decided that the music was too angry and violent, began to purvey a brand of punk that was more emotional—hence Emo (apparently anger doesn't qualify as an emotion). This hardcore rock is also referred to as Emocore. A more violent brand is known as Screamo, bringing us full circle.

Understand that it is no longer enough to dig heavy metal; you must choose from thrash metal, speed metal, or the invitingly named death metal. Even choosing this last will not suffice as you might want to specialize in melodic death metal, and even more specifically the sub-sub-sub-genre of Scandinavian Death Metal—not to be confused with, but unfortunately hard to distinguish from, black metal. (Hint: some black metal bands are associated with church burnings, murder, and National Socialism. Nice.)

If you think this is confusing, don't even consider getting involved with Electronica. This section of the few remaining brick and mortar music distributors stretches on like the corn fields of Kansas, offering genre divisions that even the cognoscenti have difficulty keeping straight: drum & bass, dub step, ambient, IDM (intelligent dance music); the apparently more intellectually challenged dance music such as: techno, house, Electro, breakbeat, trance, glitch, trip-hop, hip-hop, and on and on.

Terms like "indie" and alt-anything are equally widespread and arbitrary resulting in an option-anxiety world that is so overwhelming that you never want to listen to anything but audio-books ever again. Fear not; the good news is that it allows you to know less rather than more and still get through any interaction with a music-nerd by adhering to the following advice.

Quick conversation-ending moves:

- Disimiss all indie rock as white middle class whining.
- Dismiss all rap as black working-class whining.
- Profess an exclusive taste for Vietnamese folk-electronica.

People it is generally acceptable to like:

- Bob Dylan
- Jimi Hendrix
- Neil Young
- Joni Mitchell (mid- to late-period)
- The Rolling Stones (*Exiles on Main Street* is the only totally safe record)
- The Clash (even people who don't like punk like them)
- Radiohead
- The Pretenders (early work—Chrissie Hynde kicks ass)
- Any mixed-sex band
- Bands with no bass player

Rock and pop aficionados have become so insecure from watching their fiefdoms decay daily that the easiest thing to do is to brush off the whole idea and claim, "I gave up and am just into classical music these days."

CHAPTER EIGHT

HIP-HOP

NO, IT'S NOT "POP"

And no, it won't just go away. Like it or not, after more than two decades we can safely say that home-boys rappin' about bitches, hos, and bling is here to stay. Whites and African-Americans alike agree on two things: it is either a new art form and an emulatable lifestyle, or a blight—the despoiler of American youth of all races. If you like it you probably don't need this chapter; if you have been avoiding it like a case of the avian flu, but don't want to seem hopelessly clueless, read on. There's lots of information here; how much of it you need or want will depend on how desperate you are to appear "cooooool" to your homey friends or your kids and grand-kids.

Hip-hop started in the Bronx (where else?) with the melding of dub reggae and New York rhyme games, incorporating samples and

rhythms from soul and funk legends. One was James Brown, the late Godfather of Soul, "the hardest-working man in show business." When he wasn't doing angel dust and indulging in high-speed chases with the police, he was arguably the first rapper, inventing the riff-based grooves that are ubiquitously sampled in hip-hop. He also showed budding "gangstas" that prison was not necessarily a bad career move. Another influence was George Clinton (with Parliament, a.k.a. Funkadelic, a.k.a. Parliament Funkadelic), who, dressed in diapers, foreshadowing the sartorial elegance of rappers like Flavor Flav, and added a psychedelic element to da funk. He also employed former James Brown bassist Bootsy Collins. In fact, for instant street-cred, try interjecting the exclamation, "It's Bootsy, baby!" arbitrarily into conversation with those who presume they are hipper-than-thou.

At over twenty years old and counting, hip-hop has history. A passing knowledge of the following cast of characters (and we do mean characters) is essential:

- **Clive "Hercules" Campbell, a.k.a. "Kool Herc,"** a Jamaican immigrant who made music by using two of the same record on two turntables, picking out the most danceable drum pattern and dropping the needle back to the beginning of one as the other ends. Anyone who thinks deejay-ing takes no talent should try this sometime. (Works better with James Brown records than with Beethoven LPs).

- **Afrika Bambaataa** was a gang leader. He used the techno band Kraftwerk's music as the basis for his big hit. And you thought that the Germans weren't funky.
- **Grandmaster Flash, the DJ of Grandmaster Flash and the Furious**

Five, was a powerful DJ, social/political commentator, depicter of ghetto life, yadda, yadda . . . Hits included "White Lines" and "The Message." If you think "White Lines" is about drugs, you are right.

- **Sugar Hill Gang's** "Rapper's Delight" is one of the most used samples ever, along with the go-go bells from Run-DMC's "Peter Piper." Ecologists should be delighted with hip-hop's propensity to recycle everything.

- **Kurtis Blow** was the first mainstream hip-hop star; he claims that the "Blow" in his name refers to a body blow (yeah right). Bob Dylan appeared on one of his records—so there! He endorsed Sprite and became a theology major—go figure.

- **Run-DMC's** fusion of hip-hop and rock with Aerosmith's "Walk This Way" led an army of young white boys to feel their inner "blackness."

- **LL Cool J,** party rapper and sex symbol, was one of the first, but certainly not the last, rapper to be embraced by Hollywood. Let's see: good-looking, can talk fast, willing to shift his image whichever way the wind blows. Yep, a match made in heaven.

- **Public Enemy** represented the peak of rap as social-political statement before the musical form shifted from Black Power to Bling Power.

- **The Beastie Boys** were first group to successfully bridge the racial divide; this all-white group is enjoyed by blacks and whites alike. They had the first rap album to go to #1 on the Billboard charts, proving that puerile teenage boy humor is beloved by all the races, and that, like Elvis, white folks can still make much more money with black music than black folks.

- **Queen Latifah**—does anyone remember that she was once a rapper?

- **N.W.A**. was the first gangsta rap group ("Niggaz with Attitudes"); members included Dr. Dre, Ice Cube, and the late Eazy-E. By dying, he achieved the ultimate in hip-hop street cred. Unfortunately it is hardest type to cash in on.

The mention of Ice Cube brings us to the "ice" section of our program, including Ice Cube, Ice-T, and Vanilla Ice (contrary to rumor there is not and never was a Jewish rapper named Ice-Berg).

- **Ice Cube's** post-N.W.A. solo career included a rise in cinema and conversion to Islam. He now stars in such terrifying movie fare as *Barbershops 1–29*.

- **Ice-T,** author of the first gangsta-rap anthem, "6 'n the Mornin'," has at least managed to avoid embarrassing himself as the hardboiled detective on *Law and Order: SVU*.

- **Rob Van Winkle, a.k.a. Vanilla Ice,** was a white rapper who wowed the nation with his single, "Ice, Ice, Baby," which was included in the film *Teenage Mutant Ninja Turtles*. It was discovered that Vanilla grew up in the suburbs instead of on the streets as he had claimed, and he lost his street cred—apparently having his song in *Teenage Mutant Ninja Turtles* wasn't enough.

- **MC Hammer** broadened the appeal of hip-hop considerably with the top-selling album *Please Hammer Don't Hurt 'Em* and the song "U Can't Touch This" before he sank like a stone and went bankrupt financially. He had long since gone bankrupt artistically.

• Hammer begat **Sean John Combs, a.k.a. Puff Daddy,** who apparently had a career as a rapper before he became a fashion designer and an actor. It is perfectly okay to make fun of P. Diddy's name(s). The incarnations are as follows: Sean "Puffy" Combs, Puff Daddy, P. Diddy, Diddy. Think of it as a form of German verb declensions.

• **Wu-Tang Clan** is an affiliation of rappers obsessed with martial arts. It includes members with names like RZA, GZA, Masta Killa, Method Man, Ghostface Killah, and Inspectah Deck. As absurd as these names might seem, they make infinitely more sense than those of rappers who thought it was a good idea to name themselves Ludacris, Canibus, D Brat, Dirt Bag, Droop-E, Nelly (a man), Sicknotes, Too Short, Peedi Crack, Common, and Z-Ro. We did not make any of these up. It seems low self-esteem is a theme running through rappers' names.

• **Snoop Doggy Dogg,** a mellow (read: stoned) gangsta, progenitor of g-funk, was produced by Dr. Dre and is the creator of Snoop Dogg's dialect, wherein "for sure, my brother," becomes "fa shizzle, ma brizzle," etc. Don't try to talk like this if you come from anywhere but the 'hood. Dogg was instumental in the rise of the West Coast hip-hop that dominated the field in the mid-nineties. Along with his label-mates on Death Row Records they sold roughly three times as many records as their East Coast counterparts. The Right Coast returned in the late nineties—see Wu-Tang Clan.

- **2Pac,** a.k.a. Tupac Shakur, was a gangsta rapper shot in '96, who produced the first hip-hop double album, *All Eyez on Me.* He has since become something of a rap saint, so tread lightly on the jokes like, "If he had lived, inflation would have made him 8Pac by now."

- **Jay-Z** went from gangsta to music business mogul—not much of a leap. Extra points for knowing that the bootylicious Beyoncé is his girlfriend.

- When **Eminem** is not busy marrying and divorcing his wife, he is busy writing songs about killing her. Considered by some to be the greatest white rapper—a field about the size of pygmy basketball stars—he too has dabbled in film and received more money and critical acclaim than most black rappers. Geez, ya think it's cause he's white? Nonsense.

If you just can't hang with rap, you can still garner some street-cred by being into experimental hip-hop, as purveyed by DJs Spooky, Krush, Food, and Shadow. Just throw out words like *mash-up*, *collage*, and *musique-concrete*, and you will be home free.

CHAPTER NINE

MOVIES

I'M WRITING A SCREENPLAY, AREN'T YOU?

Hey, these days every waiter from Astoria to Anchorage is working on a "treatment of a concept of an idea based on a graphic novel for a buddy movie about a pair of Los Angeles gynecologists—sort of like *Butch Cassidy* meets *Dead Ringers*." After all, bullying your way into pictures is as old as the MGM lion. Pioneer moviemakers are now having reverential Bible-length tomes written about them even though—or because—they started out as furriers, meat merchants, and shoe salesmen. Having a BFA in "cinemah" from NYU doesn't mean doo-doo these days, either. You'll find that faking cinematic savvy is basically a cinch, once you master some simple concepts and vocabulary. Here's what you need to know.

Movies are made by directors.
In the old days they wore berets, ran around yelling "Cut!" through

megaphones, and didn't excite much attention off the set. But now, any director worth his celluloid salt drives a Mercedes and has an entourage, not to mention paparazzi. In Filmdom today, the director is it. He is the Artist, and the movie is His Work. Speak of him as an auteur (AW-toor) who writes the movie with his camera, like a novelist with a pen or a painter with a brush. That's what some French egghead critics suggested back in the fifties (among them François Truffaut and Jean-Luc Godard, who strangely enough became directors themselves—and are still two good names to throw around).

There are college curriculums devoted to scrutinizing everything from *Gone with the Wind* to Bugs Bunny cartoons for Hidden Significance. This is because directors have a Vision—they have Something to Say. (Legendary producer Sam Goldwyn, who once barked, "You want to send a message? Go to Western Union!" is spinning in his grave.) So never refer to a film by its stars or subject matter. Don't talk about "that cop movie with DiCaprio"—it's Scorcese's *Departed*, and it's "about" violence, loyalty, and the American Dream. *Some Like It Hot* isn't a Marilyn Monroe comedy, it's director "Billy Wilder at the peak of his career." And *The Lord of the Rings* trilogy is not "the cool Hobbit movies" but "Peter Jackson's overview of good and evil as seen through a phantasmagoria of imagery."

In fact, it's très chic to avoid discussing the content of a movie entirely. Just tell gossip about and/or psychoanalyze the film's director. You don't actually have to have seen Woody Allen's new movies to authoritatively dismiss them: "Allen's such a neurotic narcissist. He's been repeating himself since *Annie Hall*, and he hasn't really been funny since he split up with Diane." Or "He's still searching for the perfect female foil, only he's trying to create a newer, younger version of himself in each film."

It helps to be passionate about your favorites and least-favorites, cool about the in-betweens. You love Krzysztof Kieslowśki (Who? Exactly!). You hate Michael Bay and think Jerry Bruckheimer belongs on TV. You understand Robert Altman, but he leaves you cold, although now that he's dead, you really miss him. You can say the same about Stanley Kubrick, but use the words "visionary misanthrope." Be careful with pronunciations, and get acquainted with the proper appellations. Never speak of "Federico Fellini" or "David Cronenberg." It's "Fellini" and "Cronenberg." Conversely, mention actors and actresses, that inferior breed (Hitchcock called them "cattle") by first names and nicknames, i.e. Brad, Nicole, and Meryl.

The next important trick of the trade—a strong cinematic vocabulary. Again, talking about what actually goes on in a movie is for amateurs. You're concerned with camera work, cutting, the script, lighting, production values, the soundtrack. It's best to approach any popular movie from an oblique angle. In discussing, say, *Gangs of New York*, mention "the imaginative set design. The script is weak," but the picture is "saved by some virtuoso editing" and "flashy production values."

"Cinematography" (that's photography to you) in general, and lighting and color specifically, are safe subjects for inspiring respect in casual conversation. Besides the cognoscenti, who ever notices the lighting in a flick unless it is so bad that you can't see anything on the screen? To say you admire the "low-key lighting" in *The Godfather* is cool; to talk about the "musky, Vermeer-like interiors" in *Last Tango in Paris* is super-hip, implying that you were taking in more than Maria Schneider's boobs and Brando's behind when you saw the picture. If you did—which you didn't.

Calling attention to the scoring is also smart (who listens?), and you'll get extra points if you can think of something bright to say about the sound mix, e.g., "The mix in the second edition of *Star Wars* is vastly superior to the first." The ultimate in finesse is a reference to the print of the film itself, and that can actually give you a quick exit if you're being pinned on a movie you should have seen but didn't: "*Apocalypse Now*? Well, the print I saw was so poor I had to walk out on it."

Choose your pose—here are two:

THE SERIOUS CINEASTE

This is extremely heady turf, consisting of a kind of radical intellectualism—Film as Art, the hallowed ground where the elite meet. You read *Cahiers du Cinéma* (preferably in the original French), *Sight & Sound*, and *Artforum*. Your idea of "fun" is watching creaky D. W. Griffith silent films and analyzing their "subtext," although you're "horrified by his racism." Watching movies consisting of close-ups of blank walls for an hour is a religious experience. You talk in terms of "semiotics," "structuralism," and "pyrotechnics," as in: "The moving-camera pyrotechnics of Adam Sandler films betray a mise-en-scène that is subtextually tragic."

The word, by the way, is *film*; *movies* are *Titanic* and Bruce Willis thrillers. *Films* used to be in other languages, with subtitles—a dubbed soundtrack "distorts the director's meaning"—but now they can be by American auteurs like Scorcese, Altman, and Kubrick.

Some History for the Serious Cineaste

Jean Luc Godard's politics get in the way of his filmmaking. *Breathless* (1960) showed great promise (and Jean Seberg in a cute little T-shirt), but by *Week-End* (1967), which is the film with the huge traffic jam in it (all you have to know), he had become boring and preachy.

Fellini was a cartoonist before he became a director. (This is a little-known fact that will get you high points.) He was very fashionable but tended toward excess—witness *Satyricon* (1967), a grotesque epic about ancient Rome. *8 1/2* (1963) was a lavish, nearly incomprehensible work about a film director (guess who) with enormous self-doubt.

Kurosawa was a great Japanese film director. His work is slow but beautiful to look at and "Shakespearean in scope." Almost everybody knows that *The Magnificent Seven* was a remake/Americanization of his *The Seven Samurai,* but mention it before your fellow cineastes do.

Everyone likes François Truffaut's work, especially *Jules et Jim,* about two friends in a romantic triangle. You think he's wonderful, too, and actually liked *Mississippi Mermaid* (1969), which starred Catherine Deneuve and Jean-Paul Belmondo. The critics hated it, it disappeared without a trace, and you'll probably be the only one who's claimed to have seen it.

The Spanish director Luis Buñuel made his first film in 1928 and is the original master of cinematic surrealism. The "razor and the eye" scene in *Un Chien Andalou* is "seminal" (and as horrific as you imagine). His surreal ambition seems to have been, in later films, to turn the gorgeous Catherine Deneuve into something grotesque or bonkers—see *Belle du Jour.*

Alfred Hitchcock really is as great as is claimed. *Vertigo*, with Kim Novak and James Stewart, is his most under-appreciated film. See it and talk about it—and the art of obsessive voyeurism—endlessly. (Extra points are awarded for preferring his earlier film *Rope*, which was filmed in ten-minute takes. Extra-extra points for actually having seen it).

Stephen Frears and Neil Jordan. Yes we get them confused as well. Frears is *My Beautiful Laundrette* and Jordan is *The Crying Game* (or is it the other way around?). All you have to say is that their British films are great and their American studio productions suck.

Though not history (yet), in order to start a controversy, bring up slasher films. *Hostel* (and its sequels) and *Saw* (ditto) are filled with ingenious grotesqueries—they may be clever, but they appeal only to our basest instincts. On the other hand, the Korean director Chan-Wook Park, with his gore-fest trilogy *Sympathy for Mr. Vengeance*, *Oldboy*, and *Sympathy for Lady Vengeance*, "examines cruelty and justice in an almost existentialist manner" (except maybe in the scene in *Oldboy* in which the hero eats a live octopus).

And should you be forced to deal with American films, the following information and esoterica will get you everywhere:

Orson Welles was twenty-six when he wrote, directed, and starred in *Citizen Kane*. It is a masterpiece. His next film, *The Magnificent Ambersons*, is beautiful to look at but is very boring. *Touch of Evil* (1958) was his last great movie (despite starring Charlton Heston as a Mexican). He was from Wisconsin, was once married to Rita Hayworth, and ended up in bad wine TV commercials (back when they had wine TV commercials). He was to thought in American cinema what Marlon Brando was to action. And both of them wound up morbidly obese. (Discuss at length.)

It is okay to like late '30s and '40s American films, especially if Humphrey Bogart, Cary Grant, Bette Davis, Robert Mitchum, or Katharine Hepburn are in them—preferably some combination thereof.

They are proof that films aren't being made like they used to be. And you love "film noir." The rest is sheer entertainment—not that there's anything wrong with that—"but what do we get from them, really?"

Stick to the hard facts and don't allow the other party to talk too much—all you really have to do is mention a little-known film by a well-known director (like *The Hit* by Stephen Frears, or was it . . .) and the conversation is all yours. Trivia is really big in this package—use it. And when confronted with a film or director you don't know, merely change the subject to Orson Welles. Everyone has a theory about him.

When serious cineastes talk to each other, they often don't even understand themselves, let alone the other person. But the more obscure your lingo, the deeper you appear to be. This is where real chutzpah pays off. The advantage of this position is its great freedom of invention (there really does exist a movie called *The Film That Rises to the Surface of Clarified Butter*, so wing it!). If pressed for a clear opinion, the kind of line that's unassailable is: "The only truly contemporary cinema is coming out of Iran and China."

THE POPCORN CRITIC

This is the turf of the trendy, fashionable, fun-loving moviegoer. "I just caught *Teen Terror VII*. It has a foot in a blender scene that makes *Texas Chainsaw Massacre* look like *Bambi*!" The basic drift here is the Bad Is Good (and Awful Is Great) syndrome. You revere and revel in pure trash, precisely because it has no pretensions to art or any significance at all.

Just pick a niche and carve it out, with the accent on visceral excitement, anything truly outré, from the latest soon-to-be-remade-in English-starring-Naomi-Watts Japanese horror film to the latest Will

Ferrell or Ice Cube comedy (which some of us consider to be another form of horror film), is fair game. Try taking a stand for Jennifer Tilly as the greatest actress in Hollywood, boast of having seen *Night of the Living Dead* (the original) eight times, or proclaim director John Waters (*Pink Flamingos, Polyester*) an auteur despite his wacky exterior. If cheap thrills are your meat, your conversational zapgun is aimed at anything "serious," i.e., anything starring Liam Neeson ("How boring can you get?") or Julianne Moore ("Puts me to sleep!"). You loved *Titanic*, and Tarantino is your personal God. (Actually, liking Tarantino falls into both the Cineaste and Popcorn Critic varieties.) And the films of Rob Zombie may be gory, "but it's his worldview that will really disturb you."

To pose as any kind of film buff, use these key words. They are ambiguous enough to suggest You Know Something.

> *Overrated* and *Underrated*, i.e., Brian De Palma is overrated (because he's just imitating Hitchcock); Brian De Palma is underrated (because he's transcending Hitchcock).
>
> *Classic*, i.e. *Shaft's Big Score* is a "classic of its kind."
>
> Adjectives for: *powerful*, *major*, and *important*.
>
> Adjectives against: *thin*, *minor*, and *irrelevant*.

The granddaddy of them all is *cinematic*. Saying a movie is cinematic is like saying the sky is bluish. But it sounds impressive.

CHAPTER TEN:

BOOKS

NOTES FOR THE BIBLIOPHILE

In so many areas faking it can be chancy. You fake it in yoga class. But suppose you find yourself in a backbend and can't get out of it and have to spend the rest of your life walking like an upside-down crab? You fake it in poker. But suppose your friendly game turns serious and all of a sudden you owe someone named Viktor $20,000? You fake it in twin-engine corporate jets, but then you're 30,000 feet up with thunderheads building. But faking it in books is so *safe*. There's literally no chance of doing yourself bodily harm. So let's get right to it.

On the first level, which we will pass over quickly, you need a subscription to *Publishers Weekly* online—www.pw.com. Reading the amazon.com reviews are not enough—you need to know the next hot novel before everyone you know has pre-ordered it. The *New York Times Book Review* is still the gold standard, though it tends to skew conservative, so if you're faking it, definitely mention how bad it is and how you think the reviewers all must be Republicans. The daily *Times* reviews come out first, so be sure to confirm, with a rueful shake of

your head, that you don't *ever* fully agree with Michiko Kakutani. Why is she such a hard-ass on brilliant writers? What has *she* ever written? *The Guardian* (guardian.co.uk) is also good—and reliably leftist, just like the U.S. papers used to be—if you want to be able to chat about the next Martin Amis or Booker prize hopeful before everyone else gets it. Finally, check out bookslut.com for the next big American authors— she gets the dish from everyone.

Now master a few basics of how to discuss books you haven't read, and let the others muddle through the verities. First off, you need an obsession with any one of the following:

- The *McSweeney's* crowd.
- *The New Yorker* writers.
- Third World writers no one else has discovered yet.

As for specific titles to be dropped into the conversation, confine yourself to the latest Pynchon (the most totally unread writer of all time) and Philip Roth. Both authors are extensively reviewed "seriously," and anyone in a present-day discussion of books will have heard of them. If your companion says she loves Roth, just say, "The new book was really intense . . . I guess he's coming to terms with death." You introduce either one when someone is holding forth on the delights or horrors of a current Oprah pick. If you're found out, just say, "Oh my God, I knew that *A Million Little Pieces* was fabricated as soon as it came out. Everyone on the book blogs was trashing him. Wait, you didn't like it, did you? Did you see the thing about him on Gawker? It was so hilarious!" Either statement will clearly establish your lead and should pretty well sweep the decks, permitting you to guide the conversation back to your own "field" with lines such as:

"Those Dave Eggers writers can be overrated, but at least *McSweeney's* is anti-corporate, and who else is even bothering to branch out of the mainstream these days?"

"That new Ian McEwan in the *New Yorker* was so cool, you had to pre-order on Amazon UK. And when is Seymour Hersh's book coming out, anyway?"

"I've just read this super-interesting new story collection, but it hasn't been translated from Tagalog yet."

Once you're free to hold forth on your own choice, your companion will be too embarrassed to disagree with you when you declare:

"I'm kind of over the novel-comic hybrid."

"I don't really trust newspaper reporters any more, but *New Yorker* fact-checkers don't screw up."

"Oh, right, you don't read Tagalog. Well, it will really be a crime if no English language press picks this one up."

About any of the above, or in fact about any book that is mentioned about which you know nothing, you're safe in dropping into a convenient pool of silence, or one of the following:

"All that minutiae. Some people like it, I know. I guess it's good for our short-attention-span era."

"I'm over snarky."

"I know you think I'm being sentimental, but what about passion?"

"Whatever. Did you finish Harry Potter?"

Of course, if all else fails, just act as if you don't read contemporary literature at all. Too ephemeral, and you feel guilty when there are so many classics you never got to.

To fake highbrow you need:

- A complete set of Proust, in paperback only.

- A two-volume set of the *OED (Oxford English Dictionary)* with the slipcase discarded and both the front and back covers partially shredded. ("I know I can get it online, but the magnifying glass is so cool!")

- A few mangy-looking selections by Samuel Beckett, Virginia Woolf, Christopher Isherwood, Vladimir Nabokov, and Jane Austen.

- A Brooklyn Industries zip-up hoodie (apologize for wearing such a cliché, but it's really warm!)

- A twenty-four-inch-high stack of yellowed, backdated *Harpers.*

- Half a dozen mugs with dried coffee rings inside them.

- A pack of cigarettes—Dunhills or American Spirit—in the freezer.

- A battered old Mac—with stickers. You've worked this one to death and can't afford a new computer.

- Bookmarks from Powell's, Bluestockings, or Booktrader—or whatever indie, second-hand bookstore still exists in your city.

- Stacks of LPs and a still-working record player.

Get rid of:

- Airport thrillers
- The *Shopaholic* series
- *Einstein for Dummies*
- All issues of *Hello!, In Touch, Star,* and *Us Weekly*
- *Lost*—Seasons 1, 2, and 3 DVD set
- X-Box
- Framed posters
- Your Nikes, and anything from the Gap

All shoes should be scruffy and unevenly worn down on the heels. You definitely need glasses with chunky frames, a geek-chic hairstyle (ponytail for girls, scruff for men), an overstuffed tote bag, and many writing implements—fountain pens are especially good. Collecting antique typewriters and actually using them for correspondence is also excellent.

Food is peasant/rustic/organic: Wasa crackers or very tough, seeded bread, hummus, fruit from the greenmarket—seasonable only—and hard-to-digest, bitter greens are best. When asked to meet at a restaurant, explain you're on a budget, but you'll be happy to cook—and could your guest please bring a bottle of wine?

Ailments should be confined to eyestrain, carpal tunnel, and allergies. Nothing that you could have possibly gotten by playing sports, unless yoga or soccer.

Your sweaters can be moth-eaten, but cashmere or merino wool shows you have excellent, purist taste. Wear Levis or vintage jeans—no Sevens or other low-rider $200 denim.

Finally, don't hide your overdue bills. Pile them up in plain sight, topping the heap with a copy of *Tin House*, clearly "the" literary journal du jour.

CHAPTER ELEVEN:

LEGITIMATE THEATER

PLAYING THE PART OF STAGE BUFF WITH PANACHE

The theater is not dead, but alive and more expensive than ever. Like, $200 seats for the latest retread of a movie that wasn't that good to begin with. However, real theater, in the tradition of Shaw, Williams, and Shakespeare, is still out there. Luckily for a faker, tour buses full of sweat-suited grandmas don't attend the highbrow productions, so you really do have a lot of room to pretend you're more sophisticated than your neighbors, who shelled out a mortgage payment for *Mamma Mia!* The neat thing about affecting expertise with serious theater is that it gives you a touch of class, even a dash of old-fashioned romance. To be "into theater" is to be involved in something serious, to hearken back to the days when people discussed the latest Beckett and Fugard plays at dinner parties—not just this week's episode of *Desperate Housewives.* To "play the part" well, you just need to familiarize yourself with some important names and a bit of behind-the-scenes terminology.

ACTING

To say an actor or actress is bad or good is much too simplistic. You don't want to sound like a movie reviewer, right? Instead, focus on the actor's technique. A good actor uses technique in the same way a dancer or musician does, i.e., you don't want to see Mikhail Baryshnikov or Keith Richards counting beats, but you do want to know that they've studied this stuff, so they could twirl in the air seven times, or a rock out a really long, complicated solo. Therefore, when you're discussing, say, Kevin Kline's *Lear* (don't say "King" first—it shows your lack of familiarity with the Bard), be sure to comment on Kline's studious preparation, as well as your own familiarity with his bona fides: "He did go to Juilliard, you know." Because so many film and TV actors now do a run on Broadway for the highbrow version of street cred, you are always safe with remarks such as, "Jennifer Garner really surprised me—I thought she'd bomb as Roxanne, but she held her own pretty well." Or, if you want to sound extra cultured: "Broadway is done. I mean, Jennifer Garner in *Cyrano*? What's next? Rosanne Barr as Ophelia? How many starving Juilliard grads out there are dying to do something real? Not to mention I wish there were some new plays to get excited about—everything's a revival! It's so centered on the bottom line, like everything these days."

PLAYWRIGHTS

There actually are a number of exciting newcomers, in the vein of the Sam Shepards and Tom Stoppards of the previous generation. Actually, Tom Stoppard is still the Hot Thing on Broadway (especially after his wonderful screenwriting work). Tickets for the handsome Czech Brit's new works are always tough to get, as his directors cast dreamy young actors and often include nude scenes. Because Stoppard's work is so intellectual—full of mathematics, Russian philosophers, and short-lived political movements—no viewers are ever sure they actually understand the plays, so it is easy to speak of them euphemistically yet intelligently: "His humor is just so out there . . . I didn't know I could find the Prague Spring so funny!" Or, if you're not sure which play to talk about, you can always remind your listener, "Of course, I've been a fan since *Rosencrantz*—it made me fall in love with theater, really."

Other popular but serious playwrights are Tony Kushner ("he brought theater back from the dead"), Martin McDonagh ("brutal, Irish"), August Wilson ("not as fresh as in the '80s, but still so important") and Suzan-Lori Parks ("so intense, but hilarious").

Of the established, you like August Wilson, Edward Albee, David Mamet, and any of the now-dead greats—Tennessee Williams, Arthur Miller (though he could be "so pedantic, but that was the time"). Sidestep detractors by simply asking them, "Well, what was the last play you saw? It wasn't at the Fringe Festival, was it? Well, you can't judge by *that*."

DIRECTORS, PRODUCERS, AND COLLECTIVES

Trevor Nunn is a genius. Julie Taymor is a genius. The Wooster Group is genius (even if their work is incomprehensible). In fact, legitimate theater is so costly to produce that anyone who manages to get more than one show on the boards is almost immediately ranked with Einstein. A hip approach to talking about these artists is to introduce some personal element in your assessment.

"Philip Seymour Hoffman (Phil Hoffman) has a lot of courage to stay in New York and keep doing theater. He's really putting his money where his mouth is. And he's supposed to be such a nice guy!"

"Robert Wilson's process is the idea. You just have to look at his sketchbooks to see that."

General guidelines

Knock musicals, but not the cool ones (*Avenue Q, Spring Awakening*)—much. Stephen Sondheim is God, and it's wonderful to see his work restaged for a new generation—"That *Sweeney Todd* was like Brecht!" It is always safe to wish for the return of the "golden age" of American musical theater. Alas, however, you fear the commercialization of hip-hop has ruined it (this is safe to say about almost any dying art form, even if it doesn't make sense).

In talking of off and off-off Broadway, the party line is: "Sure there's great stuff there, but who has the time?" Of shows that move from "off" to "on" Broadway: "the ticket prices just sky-rocketed—we were really lucky to catch it downtown." Critics are stupid, but their power has waned since the Internet—make up a blog name to reference if you need to. Often, a "milestone in theatrical history" failed at the box office. Your defense? "It was too smart for the Disney crowd."

A final tip: If you're caught out having seen nothing on Broadway in the last decade: "I hardly ever leave Brooklyn. Don't tell me you *still* haven't been to BAM?"

CHAPTER TWELVE:

TRAVEL

GETTING THERE/BELONGING THERE

The good news is that the world is opening up—spas in Tibet, condos on the Black Sea, casinos in Swaziland—which means that you can almost always drop a resort name guaranteed to be unvisited by anyone present. Faking it in the resort-visiting world divides roughly into two categories: the tried 'n' true (but exclusive, of course) and the never-even-heard-of-it before.

In the first category, year in, year out, nothing beats Cap d'Antibes and Palm Beach. Shahs, princes, and ex-presidents have spent literally millions trying to displace both. They've all failed. Sure, there are good seasons and some not-so-good seasons, but by and large, the Cap and Palm are staples, names to be dropped right off in the warm-up rounds before you settle into lesser-known stuff.

Visiting regularly is good. Having a villa (not a cottage, please) is better. Of course, your own yacht affords a pleasing mobility not to be sneered at. If you have your own villa but are not in it at the moment, it's because you've lent it to close friends who needed anonymity. In

one breath, this establishes your largesse and your coterie of high-born intimates.

In the days of the great ships, snobbery was affected by means of luggage labels—six-inch-long things labeled CUNARD or WHITE STAR and backed with forever glue. These are now of course passé, and leaving the three initial luggage tags on your stuff is all too apt to result in your gear being shipped to DFW while you await it in SYD.

Where do you stay in . . .
- London? A little place near Princess Gate (with a wink).
- Paris? With a friend. Toujours.
- Rome? Have you ever seen the private apartments in the Vatican?
- Athens? I was willed a sixteenth-century villa half an hour outside the city. Ten years ago, if you'd asked me I'd have given it to you. Now, of course, I'm glad I was too busy to get rid of it.
- Peking? In the Cuban Embassy.
- Tokyo? My company keeps a little . . .

Tastes in resorts are fickle. Nassau used to be it, now we leave it to show biz and the Mob. Once upon a time Biarritz was overbooked and turning away the swells by the gross. Today it rains a lot and only Europe's blue-blooded bleeders are in summer residence.

Aspen was good until it went artsy; Puerto Vallerta was great until the iguana was imported. Mt. Tremblant was fantastic until the chef died, and it also became possible to jet off to the Alps.

The Great Barrier Reef is one of those perennials, as is the middle fork of the Salmon River. Alaska, so vast and unvisited, makes great name dropping. Any Eskimo-like word—Achoo, Tootoo, Meetu— will serve as one of those uncharted little islands where "we went to film the Kodiaks." You were flown in. Incredible scenery. "in fact, if you'd like to download my pics . . ."

Safari in Africa, once the epitome of Teddy Roosevelt-like chic, is now almost humdrum. Buses from the lodge to the feeding pride of lions depart on schedule. If your camera jammed, buy yourself a complete set of African wildlife slides as you depart Nairobi Airport.

Canoe trips up the Amazon, if it's far enough up, are acceptable and even enviable. Just be certain it's piranha season (they're harmless as minnows fifty weeks a year) and that missionaries were sacrificed there less than two years before.

Even the fabled Roof of the World—Bhutan, Sikkim, and Tibet— is being turned into revolving doors for the Nikon-bedecked tourist. But if you can allow that you stayed "at the palace" (lowercase p), it might just be worth a brief mention.

Wherever you go, you're expected to do something. Lying around on a deck chair or on a beach might have been fine a few years ago, but no more. Vacations must be verb packed.

YOU:	YOU NEVER:
salmon fish	deep-sea fish
"go" for marlin	go to ski school
hit the boards (ski)	gamble
try your luck (roulette)	take a camping trip
trek into the interior	get on this tippy platform kind of thing
raft downstream	have the s—- scared out of you by apes
snap some fantastic gorilla close-ups	throw up
crew	pay ten bucks to go down this ladder on the side of a reef
scuba	

CHAPTER THIRTEEN

NEW YORK, NEW YORK

SOPHISTICATED STREET SMARTS

There are few areas in the known world where being from New York does not place you at a distinct advantage. New York City is universally accepted as the fastest paced, most sophisticated, and exciting city extant. (Take that, Berlin, Paris, and London). "New York" used to mean only Manhattan, but now tourists seem excited to visit Brooklyn and even Queens (a borough whose sole purpose is to be on the way to Long Island, where New Yorkers go to swim), and with the constant influx of hipsters desperate for housing, those boroughs are now actually worth living in. The Bronx is "coming back" as well, although it may take some time before there will be many reasons besides the Yankees, the Zoo, and the Botanical Gardens to go there. For all intents and purposes we can still ignore Staten Island.

Please remember that New Yorkers have an island mentality. They know nothing about geography and will not know where you come from even if you show them on a map. South is downtown, north is Harlem, west is California, east is Asia, and the rest is a blur.

If you are in New York and are trying to pass, remember the following: New Yorkers hate small talk except when a complaint is involved. "Isn't it a lovely autumn day?" will peg you as an alien and get you shunned. "How do those lousy drivers from New Jersey get their licenses?" will get you a knowing smile and good tips on where to eat from cabbies. And please don't try to speak to strangers in elevators, buses, or subways—they will think you are crazy and ignore you, realizing that that you are a Dubuquer in a Manhattanite's clothing.

New Yorkers may not always be loved, but they will always be respected. If you can survive with style in New York, you can thrive anywhere else. And so if you would like the respect and awe that comes with being a New York native (or at least one familiar with everything that "is" New York) but have never been nearer the "City" than Manhattan, Kansas—and have no particular desire to do so—here are some banners you can wave. And always remember, New Yorkers can attack their city, but "foreigners" can not. Think: Bravery and pride while being blasé about both, and you've got the attitude.

First, some facts:
- There are, give or take, 8 million people living in New York City, 25 percent of whom were not born in the United States.
- Twice as many people live in Brooklyn than in Wyoming and Montana combined.
- Manhattan is 22.6 square miles.
- There are almost 10,000 licensed restaurants.
- There are 14,000 taxis.
- There are 20 million miles of telephone wires.
- Murder rate per person: 6.9 per 100,000, making it the safest large city in America.

YOU ARE YOUR NEIGHBORHOOD

New York is divided into unofficial districts well-known to the natives. You can pick your assumed point of origin to fit your own personality.

Upper East Side

(according to lower Manhattanites, anything east of 5th Avenue and north of 14th Street)

Upper East Siders are either young and upwardly mobile or older and already rich. They dress expensively but not necessarily well (even their jogging clothes are expensive—no cut-offs here). They are the establishment. If you are pretending to be from the UES, feel free to discuss futures and commodities and the long lines for movies on Friday nights (it never occurs to an Upper East Sider to go on a week-night or, horrors, a weekday). Bone up on the newest downtown restaurants and claim you can get in whenever you want because the wine guy ("sommelier" is a very '70s word) went to school with your sister/daughter (depending on your age) and his folks have a little place near yours in the Hamptons.

You have "no crime problem" but it costs you the "gross national product of a small country to park the car." You have "all the major museums within walking distance" but "never have time to go." Men wear conservative suits for business and formal occasions; women wear furs (the last place on earth that they do) as far into summer as they dare, and dress as if they are still dating at sixty. Even their hair looks expensive, and Botox is practically distributed at bus stops.

Upper West Side

(above 59th Street and west of "the Park" — Central, of course)

The UWS is like a liberal version of the UES. It is establishment with artistic pretensions. Here reside successful writers, professors, classical musicians, psychiatrists, etc. As a West Sider, you "love off-off Broadway theater" and "attend viola da gamba concerts at the local church." You "love Shakespeare in the Park." Men are either disheveled or wear tweed or corduroy suits and jackets with elbow patches, while women sport the high-fashion equivalent of earth shoes and dress as if they gave up men at thirty-five.

Hell's Kitchen/Clinton

(42nd Street to 59th Street west of Sixth Avenue)

Originally known as Hell's Kitchen for good reason, as gentrification set in, developers have tried to get people to call it "Clinton." With the usual ironic perversity of hipness, even new yuppie residents still like to call it Hell's Kitchen. Residency once imbued an air of toughness, partly due to its proximity to then-gritty Times Square. With the Disney-fication of 42nd Street, living in Hell's Kitchen just means you couldn't afford Chelsea.

Chelsea

(14th Street to 34th Street west of Fifth Avenue)

This has taken over from the West Village as the gay Mecca. It used to be that people who lived in Chelsea would have liked to live on the Upper West Side but couldn't afford it—now the reverse is true. If you are not gay, you are rich and trendy, although there's nothing wrong with being both.

West Village

(Houston to 14th Street west of Washington Square)

The West Village is not a good banner to wave if you want to get the full benefit of the New York Mystique. It has been too expensive for too long to host anyone but retired gays and 1950s-style bohemians with rent-controlled apartments who have lived there for forty years, or conservative rich people. However, claiming to have lived there since the bohemian days (provided you are old enough) will get you points as an old-school New Yawker.

SoHo

(for "south of Houston"—which is pronounced "howston"—also known more esoterically as NoCal, for North of Canal)

Claiming to be an artist from SoHo will give you away immediately as a fraud and a charlatan, as everyone from New Jersey to New Guinea knows that all the artists moved out of SoHo years ago. Claiming to be a lawyer with a multi-million-dollar co-op loft (which "seemed expensive at the time, but feels like a bargain now") will ring much truer. Name a movie star and claim he or she is "looking" in your building, but "no-one is selling—not for any price."

Tribeca

(The Triangle Below Canal)

Gentrified shortly after Soho, you must now be Robert DeNiro to live there.

East Village

(Houston to 14th Street and the Bowery to Avenue D)

You are a lawyer fresh out of college, or anyone fresh out of college with parental support. You might be an artist or a musician but only if you have lived there for twenty years. Male and female, you wear black winter and summer.

The Lower East Side

(Between Houston and Delancey, East of Broadway)

Formerly rife with discount clothing stores run by ancient Hebrews and heroin shooting galleries, this locale rose from the ashes in the nineties to become one of the trendiest areas on the island. Faking it here is almost redundant. You are an artist of some sort, or connected with the arts or pretending to be. Men must wear what they will be wearing in Williamsburg next year, and women must be darkly beautiful and seemingly unaware of it. Complain incessantly about gentrification while dining at the local, prohibitively expensive restaurant. Dumpy, walkthrough, unrenovated apartments are going for $400K.

Williamsburg

(Brooklyn, along the "L" subway line)

Once the province of Hassidic Jews, this section of Brooklyn is living proof that people tend to settle along the railroads. The first few stops outside of Manhattan on the "L" quickly became a destination for the terminally hip pioneers with insufficient funding to live in the East Village. Safer than the Lower East Side, it was gentrified first. Forget claiming residence if you are over thirty-five. If you are young enough to carry it off, you must affect the latest in boho fashion and complain about the "reverse bridge and tunnel traffic from Manhattan, clogging up the clubs and restaurants on weekends." Tons of new large Thai restaurants and pricey wine bars. And when the Williamsburgers have kids and can't eat all of that spicy Thai food anymore, they move to Park Slope (if they have a closetful of money), and cram the streets with $900 double-wide strollers and walk their Labradoodles in Prospect Park.

Astoria, Queens; Harlem; and the **Bronx** are where the next generations of pioneers are settling. Claiming you live in any one of these areas will truly impress hip people from New York but may confound out-of-towners.

You now know all you need to know about New York City. And that, as any true New Yorker will tell you, is all you need to know.

CHAPTER FOURTEEN

ARCHITECTURE

THE WORLD OF STICKS, STONES, STEEL, AND GLASS HOUSES

First of all, before you can hope to act with panache in the company of architects, you have to own the right glasses. Then it is essential to recognize the Prime Factor that overshadows every other consideration in the life of any architect. *Frustration.* Pure. Unalleviated. Nonstop.

An architect, like the unicorn, is a creature of misconception. The function of someone who describes herself as a builder is unquestioned. One rock atop another, and soon there's your little house on the prairie. Where was the architect? Um, nowhere.

An architect is haunted by the niggling suspicion that he may be unnecessary, and may, like an unpleasantly clogged artery, simply be bypassed. In fact, very often he is bypassed. All of his biggest and best ideas end up getting the kibosh once construction is underway: they're too expensive, too risky, and won't accommodate the developer's need for parking, retail space, and anti-terrorist barricades.

Of course, this is nothing new. The pyramids, the Great Wall of

China, the Roman catacombs, even the Empire State Building—name the architect. See? There must have been several for each, since these projects took years—centuries?—to complete. Now, of course, architects get top billing, though the most famous can often only show a handful of completed, successful, leak- and crumble-free projects. And yet, to arrive at this non-status status, consider what's involved. Four years of college, three more in architectural school, a couple more as a gofer, and then what can the newly arrived architect expect to find? Probably unemployment.

For a fortunate few, there's a long, gray future consisting of a kitchen stool, a drawing board, T square, and Mac, and the chance—if the firm gets the contract—to design the profile of a girder that will support the overhang of a millionaire's bathroom pipes. The lives of architects are slog-along existences, replete with groins and quoins, with pediments and plinths. Any hopes they might harbor of getting to design the next Sydney Opera House or Guggenheim Johannesburg are about as realistic as hoping that Prince William will decide to move into the house next door to you in New Jersey.

Contrast this to the life of a law student: by the end of three years, she can—if she's gone to an Ivy, aced her exams, and studied hard enough for the bar—guarantee that she'll be making a quarter of a million dollars a year by the time she's thirty (of course she'll have no life, will have no time to spend all that money, and will owe her first ten year's salary back in student loans, but who's counting?). Or an MBA. If he does everything by the book, downs shots on Friday afternoons with the right hot dogs, golfs with the hot dogs' bosses, and manages to keep from insider trading, he'll own a square block of Park Avenue before too long. But an architect . . . After having been a sneakier analytical thinker than the law student, a bigger math nerd than the MBA, and better at drawing than anyone he ever met, he might make money when he's fifty. Until then, he'll have to shell out for Japanese clothing and German eyeglass frames to even look the part enough to get in the running for jobs.

Therefore, while it may be tempting to make fun of architects for their pallor and affinity for Dutch engineering, they're really all smarter than the rest of us, and they manage to look really good while being so. If you can fake some of that intelligence at parties, then no one else will have any idea whether you're right or not. Because architecture is so theoretical, so vocabulary-heavy, that even other architects don't always understand what their colleagues are nattering on about.

"Less is more," said Mies van der Rohe (who is to architecture what Rin Tin Tin is to canine heroics), not knowing how squarely he was coming down on the head of the architect's tack.

Architects adore tossing words around in this quasi-meaningless style. They frequently speak of honesty, purity, strength, integrity, and tonality. They're not talking of religious conversions, of love affairs, or moral doctrine. They're talking about walls, floors, roofs, ceilings, and downspouts.

Every American architect has One God: Uncle Frank. You can love him, you can hate him, you just can't ignore him. If you decide you're pro-Frank Lloyd Wright, you're seriously concerned with the sincerity of Falling Water, the Price Tower, and Taliesin West.

- They speak to you.
- They represent an ineffable balancing of void and bulk.
- They represent certain essential syntactical nuances—
  plus, they're so pretty!
- They render obsolete all seminology of infrastructure.
  Or they don't. Either way is okay.

If you find yourself closeted with FLW freaks, no problem. Stretch your verbal wings and soar. But what if you've fallen in with the antis, the cons, the nay-sayers? Still no problem. The anti-Frank Lloyd Wright school of architecture consists exclusively of a single, supersterile, high-minded German: Walter Gropius. It was he who founded something called the Bauhaus (pronounced "bowhowse") school of architecture. It's fair to say that the Bauhaus was/is to architecture what Othello is to wife abuse.

Wright hated Gropius. Gropius hated Wright.

It's up to you to choose one and conspicuously ignore the other. Since both Wright and Gropius are safely dead, you can feel free to interpret the work of either one more or less on your own terms, provided you confine yourself strictly to a vocabulary that is nonconcrete. Rather, keep it airy. Avoid facts. Avoid, for instance, hazarding a guess as to the height of any building, the purpose for which it was constructed, or even whether or not it still stands.

While history (or faking a knowledge of history) is important, the Wright/Gropius debate is old news compared with the latest architectural feuds and trends. How high is too high? Is private development less pure than public works? And—most of all—Frank Gehry: has he ruined architecture forever? You don't really need answers to any of these questions. A few assurances that you find Tokyo compelling (or overrated), would love to go to Dubai (or think it's a travesty), and couldn't *stand* Bilbao (or couldn't help finding it just plain fun), will work in most social situations.

In case you find yourself talking to someone who actually knows about specific architects, here is a quickie primer on the other big names:

Daniel Libeskind was the winner of the new World Trade Center competition. Of course, his ideas have been unbearably altered by the site's philistine owners. Libeskind's genius is in his desire for preservation and communication in his work. He designed the Holocaust Museum in Germany and brought some of the same ideas about remembrance to bear on his designs for the Freedom Tower in lower Manhattan. Obviously, as his buildings have commemorated such dark events, you will not have a hard time faking knowledge through the use of serious expressions and musings about the "inhumanity" of local government.

Rem Koolhaas. Just getting his name right will already put you ahead of the game. As the designer of Prada stores in New York and LA and the Guggenheim Las Vegas, you don't really need to know what his work looks like to have an opinion: showy. But a guilty pleasure.

Maya Lin. After designing the Vietnam Veteran's Memorial when she was still a Yale undergrad, Lin has gone on to design a sculpture commemorating women at her alma mater, a Civil Rights Memorial, and several other sculptures and installations in that vein. As one of the few "name" women architects, you are safe in simply referring to her as "very, very special." Then shake your head softly.

That should be enough to get you through even the longest evening of architecture-talk. If you're still nervous, go back and watch some films about greats now gone: Louis Kahn (underrated in his own time); I. M. Pei (Japanese—and actually still alive, though quite old), and designer of the infamous Louvre Pyramid—you can't understand why everyone didn't love it immediately; Philip Johnson (wore big glasses, built Glass House). In a bind, you can always switch the subject over to "green" building. Everyone knows it's happening, but no one knows where or how.

CHAPTER FIFTEEN:

HORTICULTURE

THE GREENING OF YOUR THUMB

"Why should I even bother trying to fake it into the earthy, fertile world of the green and the growing? For only a little more effort I could pass myself off as an astronaut, a reader of the Rosetta Stone, or a polo player. There's no percentage in it."

Wrong.

The payoff for successfully faking it as a horticulturist—a person beloved for composting and mulching, for staking up and cutting back—is subtle but definite. Pass yourself off as a horticulturist, and at once you sprout an image that is as likable as it is useful. There is something about someone who grows veggies that just makes unthink-

able any suggestion of serious wrongdoing.

Your moods and quirks—especially your quirks—will be indulged. You hate your neighbor? The lady who lives opposite you? The kid on the next block? Feel free to say so. Loving zinnias and rutabagas as you do, you're allowed to wallow in strong dislikes in other areas, and with as much verve as you'd like.

You begin with a pair of rubber-soled, supersensible shoes—L.L. Bean duck shoes are ideal, but any old pair of flat, ugly shoes will do. Get them well caked with good, wet dirt (hereafter known as soil), dry them carefully on a piece of newspaper, and once the stuff is hard as iron, drop the shoes just behind your front door. Granted, this introduction to the haute monde of horticulture is more effective if you don't live in an apartment. But even if you do live in an apartment, follow through. Even the most heartless of concrete-and-steel cities have public parks, botanical gardens, and even the odd roof plot, all of which, as a horticulturist, you frequent.

Save enough of this same soil to fill several flats (the gardener's term for poorly constructed oblong wooden boxes about three inches deep). Put the flats in plain view on your window sill and never mind that you have nothing growing in them. In those flats you are starting seeds.

"What kind of seed?" For this one, you dip back into your high school Latin; just about anything you can manage to retrieve therefrom will do the trick. "Mea culpa japonnicus." "Ignobile vulgus alba."

Seed catalogs are usually free, but even if not it pays off to spend a few bucks in order to have a good fat collection of these full-colored, lavishly illustrated booklets. Stack them on chairs and tables in your living room. Having the cream of the crop of catalogs but choosing to bypass them is even better. You're sick and tired of what they have to offer, so this year you're having "just about everything sent over from a little nursery man you know in the Cotswolds country in England."

Muddy shoes, boxes of only dirt, seed catalogues in ample evidence—that's a good start but certainly not enough. Somewhere along the line you're going to have to have a plant or two to substantiate your high rank in the horticultural hierarchy. For this we recommend the following. Acquire from your local supermarket—especially right after Christmas—one of those woebegone poinsettia plants. Failing that, get yourself a hard-nosed, stiff-limbed rubber plant. If that isn't totally indestructible, it's the next thing to it.

Take it home and lop off the branches on one side of it, right at its waistline. Now take one of those lopped-off branches, peel away any foliage. (You now have an unidentifiable plant.) Finally, take a foot or so of ordinary gauze bandage and tie the butchered-up limb back onto the waist of the parent plant.Of course it looks funny. A plant with a bandaged middle. But it's exactly what you want.

"That bandaged plant over there near the window? Oh, no, it's not bandaged at all; it's a graft I'm starting. A friend at the Department of Agriculture wanted to know if I could come up with a disease-resistant peach tree. That's just one of several I'm trying out for them."

If you're not really into the finer points of housekeeping, passing yourself off as a horticulturist is right up your alley. Slightly soiled slipcovers, frayed-out rugs, and tabletops with cigarette burns and glass rings all over them are all right in character. It's not the house you care about after all, it's the garden.

Brag about the fact that even though you live in a Zone 4 (there are 12 – from coldest to warmest), you can grow Rosemary (normally found in 6 or above). Why? Well, you're being helped by Global Warming, of course, but you've also found the latest in mulch and wind protection. Tomato plants all year round? Of course—you wrap the tomato frames in old cashmere sweaters. And haven't we all grown tired of pachysandra, that okay ground cover that's all over? Well, you've discovered Vinca Minor. It's slow growing, but the lavender flowers are sooooo charming and the cover lasts the whole year!

Now what if you have no garden? It's because (sigh) you spend all your time running around as a consultant to other people who want to know if they should replace all their privet with hemlocks or whether to turn their artificial goldfish pond and waterfall into a Shakespearean herb garden.

As a horticulturist, you're free to wear the most disreputable clothes—the more raggedy, the better. Men should specialize in baggy corduroy trousers, out-at-the-elbow cardigans, and plaid flannel shirts with missing buttons. For women, the uniform is built upon wraparound canvas skirts with pockets spacious enough for balls of twine and clippers. Top things off with mismatched, mothy Shetlands and gloves that look as though they'd been buried by a puppy after being well chewed.

Casual cocktail conversation should be peppered with mention of ground covers and mulching. Talk about hybridizing (the botanical equivalent of breeding a horse to an ass and getting a mule), hydroponics, succulents, aphids, and bag-worms at the dinner table, and you'll be on fertile ground.

Never hesitate to load up at farm stands with strawberries, asparagus, Boston lettuce, and kumquats. Take them home, dump them out of the original containers, and rewrap them in your local newspaper, taking care to make untidy, soggy packages. Hand these out liberally to friends you wish to impress. The more out of season the offering, the better—tomatoes in December, radishes in February. You grew them all under lights in your bathroom.

Finally, try to remember whenever it's a particularly lovely day—sunny, mild, clear as a bell—to respond to any appreciative comment about the weather by saying, "Well, yes, of course, if you don't care about the water table." Since no one has ever seen a water table, you're 100 percent safe in assuming that it has not been given a thought. "The water table," you tell this feckless horticultural ignoramus, "is really down. A nice sunny day is okay if you're only interested in playing golf. But what we really need is a good solid week of steady rain." Conversely, during a downpour, while everyone else is moaning, squishing around in bubbling shoes and soaked-through clothing, you be sure to let it be known that "we really need this rain. Have you any idea how low the water table is this month?"

CHAPTER SIXTEEN:
GETTING IN SHAPE

LET'S GET PHYSICAL

Even if your most strenuous activity is getting in and out of a taxi cab, you can fake it in the world of health and fitness. Just follow this three-step Guaranteed No-Sweat Fitness Program. Remember to take each step slowly. Rome wasn't built in a day and neither was Arnold Schwarzenegger.

STEP 1—ATTITUDE. OBTAIN ONE. A FIERCE ONE.

This first and most important step is designed to give you confidence through simulated bravado. It doesn't matter that it's false. It just matters that you act tough. In order to be tough you must think tough, so go out there and purchase the theme from Rocky and Van Halen's entire box set. Nothing says "I'm fit" like sitting around the house listening to cheesy '80s Van Halen power chords. Play them incessantly for inspiration. Realize that true fitness freaks don't have time to socialize—they're too busy running, spinning, hefting weights, power yoga-ing, and swimming laps to go anywhere else. The chances, therefore, are pretty slim of your encountering a bona fide gym-rat who isn't totally preoccupied with his activity or too out of breath to carry on a decent conversation. Fear not—you will be able to hold your own in normal circles, where conversation is preferred over perspiration.

STEP 2A—MEN

Gents, you've got to look the part. Squelch your immediate impulse to splurge on the latest designer warm-up suit, tennis togs, or nifty little shorts with built-in-underpants. Only the nouveau male jock has a closet full of color-coordinated tops, bottoms, and footwear. The true jock, which is, of course, what you aspire to simulate, began working out long before the gym-dandy look became fashionable. What you want is a set of real cotton "sweats." Anything else will brand you a hopeless dilettante. Your serious sweats should be pure gray (easily accomplished), ill fitting (ditto, they are all, naturally), torn, worn, and sweat-stained to symbolize the "pain" you've been through. This last criterion is not so easy to meet, as there's nothing like raw, unadulterated sweat. If you, therefore, must wear a new sweat suit, at least remember to remove the price tag and wash it in hot water with a box of rocks at least 100 times and proceed to sleep in them for a few months to obtain the efficient odor quotient. Then bemoan the fact that your old smellies just simply finally "fell apart, the poor things, after all I put them through."

Depending upon your chosen specialty or locale, you can—and

should—supplement your basic grays with the acceptable accessories. Runners, for instance, can enliven the overall ensemble with sneakers in colors that nice people never knew existed, let alone dreamed they'd some day be putting on their feet. Tennis players (or any racquet-sport enthusiast) can add a tasteful wristband. Leg warmers—these must be squashed uselessly around your calves and ankles—lend a dancerly panache to an otherwise dull picture.

You must, of course, wear your sweat suit everywhere—to the supermarket, the hairdresser, the movies, and cocktail parties—in order to cultivate the impression that your life and your day revolve around your workouts and you "just don't have time to change—life is so much simpler this way, isn't it?" Your misshapen grays will cover up a multitude of sins. Since everyone looks like a sack of potatoes when thus attired, no one will know that underneath lurks not the well-defined body of chiseled muscle marbled with pumped-up veins, but the first prize winner in the Jell-O lookalike contest.

Failing the acquisition of the aforementioned disgusting garments (or to augment their effect), a "sports-related injury" is a must. Making your entrance on crutches can always be done with sporty style, especially if you can introduce your companion as your massage therapist. But a strategically placed ace bandage (say, on the knee) and a stoic "Don't worry—the arthroscopic surgery was a huge success" will always do in a pinch. Make sure you are prepared with a story of torn ligaments, pulled tendons, and bits of dislodged cartilage, because your plight will become the hot topic of the evening. Don't forget to bring your own conveniently portable and pleasantly theatrical IcyHot topical pain reliever in case it "acts up."

If you just can't get out of a conversation about working out, feel free to wax rhapsodic about your newfound obsession with "spinning." In this activity, reminiscent of being press-ganged onto a slave galley, an instructor barks encouragement at a room full of sweating souls mounted on stationary bikes, exhorting them to new depths of exhaustion.

Or extol the virtues of free-weights over Nautilus machines, "The act of self-stabilization works so many more muscles." Fortunately it also causes more injuries (see earlier).

STEP 2B—WOMEN

Much like anything in life, the exact opposite is true for the female fitness apparel set. True female fitness fanatics take great pride in their exercise ensembles. A sensational workout wardrobe is the mark of the professional in Pilates classes everywhere.

The more color-coordinated, celebrity-inspired, and designer-labeled you can get yourself, the better. Nothing, and we mean nothing, says female fitness maven like the ass-stretching signage of Juicy Couture. Browse bookstores in it. Sit down in Starbucks for five hours and read *The Bridges of Madison County* in it. Down entire batches of raw chocolate chip cookie dough in it.

But for God's sake get it dry-cleaned. Those catty girls at the gym are watching your every move. Do not—we repeat—DO NOT show up in gray sweats. The fitness Nazis are waiting to nail your Target-Inspired sassy self to the stairmaster and ask questions later. Leave the bulls-eye at home ladies.

STEP 3—THE LINGO

Fortunately for you, the world of fitness is filled with words and phrases that can easily be incorporated into any conversation, during any situation. With a little imagination they will not only impress your friends and relatives, but also get you out of many an embarrassing moment.

Carbohydrate Loading, a.k.a. Carb Loading for those with precious few moments for syllables on their hands. Before a competition, athletes stuff themselves with foods rich in starches and sugars to increase their energy. This provides you with a handy way out should you be caught red-handed in the spaghetti pot: "You don't think I want this third helping of fettucini, do you? I have to eat this—I'm carb loading, you know."

Protein Building. The fettuccini-thon mentioned above conveniently provides a reason to unabashedly gorge yourself on meatballs and sausages, because any athlete worth his weight in amino acids knows that proteins are the building blocks for muscles.

Hitting the Wall. Though this may sound exactly like something you'd like to do with the next iron-pumper you meet, it is actually the excruciating moment at which a marathoner's muscles finally run out of energy (usually before the twenty-mile mark). Use this catch phrase during any relatively long-distance event such as standing up or sex: "Gee, my legs feel as though I've hit the wall." Or, "I guess I still haven't recovered from the last time I hit the wall."

Peaking. During the last few days of a training period, athletes perform less work but at a higher intensity. This is supposed to achieve that elusive, delicate point in their development during which they are performing at their mental and physical best, called "the peak." Should your companion's words or actions threaten to upset your (nonexistent) peak, scream at the top of your lungs, "Not now—I'm peaking."

Electrolyte Replacement. Every runner worth his salt pills knows that exercise creates an electrolyte imbalance in the muscles. Thus beer, which is rich in electrolytes, can and should be swilled with heady abandon. Between chugs, you say, "Of course I don't normally quaff three pitchers at one sitting—but I must replace my electrolytes or I'll really be in trouble."

Fast Twitch, Slow Twitch. Sprinters have an abundance of fast-twitch fibers in their muscles for speed; marathoners have more slow-twitch fibers for endurance. The next time you miss a bus because you couldn't hoist yourself off the bench while clutching your Krispy Kreme, you have an excuse ready: "We long-distance runners can't have too many fast-twitch fibers, you know." If under certain "circumstances" you've performed too quickly, it's "because we sprinters never will win prizes in the slow-twitch department."

Runner's High. Enough has been written about this state of euphoria already. You can use this term to explain away nearly any erratic, but happy, behavior.

Bonking. Not to be confused with runner's high (or boinking for that matter), this condition occurs when the liver runs out of fuel and is characterized by shakiness, dizziness, confusion, and lack of coordination. It is often easy to confuse bonking with the advanced states of physical and mental deterioration seen at cocktail parties in full swing. (Note: It is possible to "bonk" and "hit the wall" at the same time.)

LSD. Completely unrelated to Timothy Leary, it is the terminally cute abbreviation for Long, Slow Distance, as opposed to sprinting.

Psychocybernetics. This refers to the mental rehearsal, akin to self-hypnosis, that jocks perform to prepare themselves before competition or during a workout. If you're ever caught staring off into never-never land, look stunned and mildly annoyed as you mutter impatiently "psychocybernetics . . . mmm."

Core Training/Core Stability/Core Strengthening. Core-anything basically talks to the folks who believe you need a strong set of abs to support the human spinal column to do much needed things like sitting in a desk chair. Luckily, many core training moves include sitting still and tightening the stomach area and not much else. So when found lounging on the couch in front of the Discovery channel watching a zebra munch a leaf, you can always claim that you're "cultivating your core."

Should all this faking of fitness leave you as limp as Frank Shorter's T-shirt, don't give up. Even when you're lying face down in a crumpled heap, you can always proclaim, "Me? Don't be silly. Of course I'm alright. I'm an Inner Athlete."

CHAPTER SEVENTEEN:

THE ART OF YOGA

PRETZEL LOGIC

Yoga is all about the art of looking Zen and looking like you might have some money. You needn't worry about actually being Zen, embracing Eastern values, or having a savings account. Regardless of the fact that you're tooling around town in your Pinto (which we suggest you hide in subterranean parking lots whenever possible), you can still stride around the neighborhood looking as if you just stepped out of the latest Ashanti Yoga class if you stride with three critical accoutrements:

THE YOGA MAT

The yoga mat is the number one most important piece of gear that you will own and not use. They can be purchased almost anywhere these days, from health food stores to Walmart to the corner gas station. Yoga mats come in an array of colors, mostly varying shades of pastel.

Pastel is Zen. Red with black polka-dots is not. Once you've acquired your mat, simply roll it into a tight bundle and prop it under your armpit. This frees up your hands for the other two less critical but very important yoga props.

THE DESIGNER COFFEE

We don't care if your favorite coffee is Folgers with flavor crystals. You're going to have to go out and purchase a designer iced coffee in a plastic cup from Starbucks or The Coffee Bean at least once, because you need the trendy see-through cup and straw to carry. As these things are plastic, you can take them home after each use, wash them, and fill them up in your own home with your own cheap coffee. When people ask you what you're drinking be sure to give the yoga lover's triple-threat: "Oh, this is a non-fat soy decaf with a cinnamon sprig." Soy, decaf, sprig. Make an index card.

THE CELL PHONE/SCOWL

You can't just waltz around town with your freshly purchased mat, non-caffeinated coffee, and a smile and expect people to take you seriously. Wipe that silly grin off your face, cultivate an air of superiority and disinterest, and get on the horn. You don't have to actually call anyone on your cell phone, just improvise. Occasionally roll your eyes, preferably when people look directly into them.

Yoga is based on a series of poses, so it's important to have a few key phrases in your pocket to sprinkle into conversation should someone ask you about your yoga mat from which we hope you have remembered to remove the price tag. You needn't know what they mean or how to bend yourself into them. We don't want you cracking a rib or banging your head on the TV stand. Take a day or two to familiarize yourself with these three sentences.

"So I did my sun salutations this morning."

"I wanted to stay in child's pose forever."

"I love downward facing dog."

Avoid the trap of finding humor in that last one. We know you're tempted. But yoga is serious business, devoid of smiles and wit. Make the mistake of cracking a downward facing dog joke and they just might kill you, wrap you in your mat, and toss you in the Far East river.

For serious Yoga one-upmanship (admittedly not a very Zen attitude) you can purport to having moved on to Bikram Yoga. This is yoga performed in a room heated to 105 degrees with 40 percent humidity. You don't ever actually want to do this, as it involves working hard in a room so hot that by the end of the session you would have to wring your underpants out.

To imply that you do this, you must drop terms like "wicking fabrics." These fabrics apparently somehow "wick" the sweat away from your body and "keep you dry for hours." We are not entirely sure how this is done or why, just as we are not sure why doing yoga in a 105-degree sweatbox is better than doing it on a very cool and airy veranda, but there you have it.

You should be aware that Bikram Yoga involves a series of 26 postures. All of the postures, except the last, are done in twos, so if you don't get it right the first time, you always have a second chance to try again—which you rarely get in life. The great thing about Bikram Yoga is that when you get tired and want to lie on your mat and play dead, no one cares. This sort of thing is actually encouraged, especially if you're looking like you might vomit.

In short, if there was ever anything you would want to fake rather than do—this is probably it.

CHAPTER EIGHTEEN:

TENNIS

ELBOWING YOUR WAY TO NET RESPECT

You'll want to fake both your ability on the court and your knowledge of the game, but the tennis world is so full of know-it-alls and done-it-alls that you can only count on very brief periods of successful deception.

YOU, THE CHAMP MANQUÉ

Tennis has ballooned to such proportions all over the world that there's almost no place left on Earth where you can be absolutely safe from being challenged to show your stuff on some nearby court. However, you should be fairly safe from actually playing in any of the following situations:

- 32,000 feet up on a transatlantic flight.
- On a coffee break talking to a fellow juror of an impounded jury, empaneled for a complex drug smuggling/murder trial.
- Visiting a sick friend in the hospital.
- Talking to somebody's grandmother, but only if she's in a wheelchair or using a walker.

If you're winging it within even 50 miles of a half-decent court, you'd be well advised to have one foot swathed in a heavy overlay of bandages, and walk with a crutch. (It's a nasty sprain, the result of running down a drop shot in Boca.)

However, if some insensitive, pushy type insists on hitting with you on a specific date, don't lose your cool. Take a deep breath and say:

- "I'd love to, but I'm playing a pro-am that day."
- "I'd love to, but I've promised Jimmy (Connors) that I'd spend (stated date) with Andy (Roddick) to see if I can help the kid with his backhand."
- "I'd love to, but I've just been scoped (arthroscopic surgery) on my (knee, shoulder), and am still in PT (physical therapy)."

YOU, THE EXPERT

To establish your undeniable intimacy with the game and its greats, you should be alert to any possibility of working the following into your conversations:

- Your great-grandfather learned tennis from none other than Britain's Arthur W. Gore, who, when he was forty-one years old, won the men's singles at Wimbledon (1909).
- You ghosted the writing of Rod Laver's Education of a Tennis Player, but you don't necessarily think that the Rocket could beat Roger (Federer).

Since a good offense is often the best defense, both on and off the court, the following information will enable you to lob verbally in any conversation, and allow you to hit that overhead smash that will put an end to any tennis-related chat and win you the discussion point.

THE DEWEY DECIBEL SYSTEM?

Young female tennis stars are either too young or too busy to have sex. Therefore, their coaches (usually their fathers or father figures) have trained them to release an orgasmic yelp each time they strike the ball. It began with Monica Seles, the phenom whose career was halted when a German Steffi Graf fanatic thrust a knife into her back. The lioness ululated into the Wimbledon Hall of Vocal Hysterics in 1992, when the formidable Martina Navratilova joined the many who had complained about her screaming. The current reigning screech queen is Maria Sharapova—who Bud Collins, sportswriter extraordinaire, has labeled Shreikapova—and was clocked at 103.7 decibels at the 2007 Wimbledon. You'll always sound in the know if you mention that you carry a set of earplugs to all the majors.

GREAT MOMENTS IN TENNIS INJURIES

Vomiting: Andy Murray at the 2005 U.S. Open and Pete Sampras in the 1996 U.S. Open put on a lovely display of on-court barfing.

The Greatest Injury That Never Was: Justine Henin, the Little Belgian Who Could, retiring in the second set of the 2006 Australian Open final because of an insisted upon—but highly unverified—stomach problem. Oddly, it caused her neither to heave, nor to leave, for a bathroom break.

THE ALL-TIME GREATEST?

Unlike boxing, which already has its greatest, tennis debate still rages as to who's the best of them all, now that Switzerland's Roger Federer and his precision tennis have swept the globe. Prior to the Open Era (1968), contenders included Don Budge, Jack Kramer, and Pancho Gonzales. But contemporary man has a short memory. Rod Laver, Pete Sampras, and Bjorn Borg are all on the current short list. However, if Federer beats Pistol Pete's Grand Slam record (14 wins) and wins the French Open (Roland Garros), there will be little arguing that he's the man.

If you want to avoid this conversation entirely, just give your vote to Martina Navratilova, who retired for the final time at the age of 49 and has more wins than Britney Spears has breakdowns.

THE FASHIONISTAS

Whether your workout gear is manufactured by Nike, Reebok, Fila, or Lacoste, dropping tennis fashion nuggets will convince everyone that you have the gift of garb:

- Rafael Nadal, the Spanish hotty who rules the clay courts with his bulging biceps and tsunami-sized topspin, is Federer's only nemesis. He changed tennis style forever with his capris and sleeveless shirts.
- The Williams sisters (Venus and Serena) may be the most innovative and worst dressed pair to have ever made a name for themselves. Since they both want careers in fashion, pray that they never retire from tennis.
- Andy Roddick's career went downhill when he switched his endorsement contract to Lacoste from Reebok. Plus, he's had dismal first-round exits in the French Open. Andy should give up the Champagne and quiche and switch back to chips and beer if he wants to succeed on the court.

THEY'RE TAKING "OVA"

Women's tennis always seemed to be dominated by Americans and Western Europeans. When you think of the greats, the following names come to mind: Williams, Williams, Evert, King, Graf, Court, Sanchez-Vicario, Henin, Capriati, Hingis. But times change, and now, the power is moving to Eastern Europe, namely Russia and the Czech Republic.

It all started when Boris Yeltsin, the first-ever popularly elected leader of Russia, took up the game in 1989 at the tender age of 58. As he appeared on the courts with racket in hand, the Russian media embraced the Grand Slam events. Whether the boom stimulated the sport's popularity or merely served as an aphrodisiac, we'll never know.

It all began with the first "ova," Martina Navratilova (the letters "ova" are added to a father's surname to indicate a female), who dramatically changed the way women trained for the game. The next "ova" was Anna Kournikova, the Queen of downloads and embodiment of a legendary Nabokov title character. We now have such established and up-and-coming supernovas as Sharapova, Kuznetsova, Vaidisova, Petrova, Hantuchova, Safarova . . . and the list ain't ova yet. The dominance of these women will be earning them ovations for a long time to come.

Learn your lessons wisely, and you can master the verbal volleying of tennis. With your trendy topspin, bantering backspin, and scintillating sidespin, you can be the spin doctor who can match anyone point for tennis point.

CHAPTER NINETEEN:
COMPUTERS

GETTING YOUR DATA TOGETHER

This is a tough one. The world of computers rearranges itself so quickly that it makes the changes in pop music seem glacial. The archetypical joke is that you go into the computer store and there is a big trash bin by the front door. You purchase your new, state-of-the-art tower or laptop and throw it in the trash on the way out of the store because by then it is obsolete. By the time this book hits the stores, Bill Gates may own the Northwest United States and be demanding that Africans who want his cure for AIDS use Windows. Or Steve Jobs might be introducing a wireless chip that goes in your brain and plays iTunes. Still, there are certain verities that, if pronounced with enough panache, will make you sound like someone conversant with computers.

The computer world is divided into two camps, and will no doubt remain so for the foreseeable future: PC and Mac. Even though PC is short for "personal computer," it generally refers to products based on the Windows operating system proffered by the aforementioned Mr. Gates's Microsoft company. Mac refers to the Macintosh computers flogged by Apple, using their own proprietary operating system. The two worlds have come much closer together. Windows Vista OS (operating system) bears a disturbing resemblance to the Mac OS, and the Macs now incorporate the Intel chips formerly used only in Windows systems, as well as offering the option to run Windows itself on a Mac. Nevertheless, some ready quips about the differences will help make you seem a card-carrying member of one group or the other.

All you need to seem PC proficient is to complain copiously about viruses. For the truly uninitiated, a computer virus is a bug that enters your computer through a corrupted file that you install or something you download from the Internet. It then wreaks havoc with your computer's functionality. PC owners are constantly dealing with pesky invaders despite erecting things called "firewalls" and installing programs that are supposed to protect them from said bugs. Mac users rarely suffer from this problem. Why, you ask? Regardless of what Apple might have you believe, it is not through the superiority of their product. It is because the people who perpetrate these viruses upon the unsuspecting public find it easier to program the little devils for Windows than they do for the Mac OS. Also, since Windows is far and away the more widely used system, they find that they can cause more damage this way. Knowing this little tidbit will go a long way toward establishing your computer cred.

Mac owners don't get off unscathed, however. In exchange for leading relatively virus-free lives, they must deal with the constant upgrading of the Mac OS system. From Panther, to Tiger, to Leopard, it is no accident that these systems are named for cruel, dangerous, capricious animals. Due to Apple's unfortunate habit of neglecting to supply their latest system to the makers of third party software until the last possible moment before release, Mac owners find that for a long time after installing the latest system—*none of their software works properly!* This is not just for the big new feline-named major systems, but for each decimal point improvement of said system until the new one arrives. To add insult to injury, Apple stalwarts must often pay for software upgrades to match the latest major system change.

To sum up, if you want to purport to be PC proficient, just lament your virus problems and claim you are too distraught to discuss it. If you wish to appear an Apple advocate, rant about how the latest version, 22.6.8, is so much worse than 22.6.7, and you wish you had stuck with 21.0! It is always acceptable to feign such frustration that you are seriously considering joining the other camp.

CHAPTER TWENTY:

ASTROLOGY

WHAT'S YOUR ... OH, NEVER MIND

Never mind about what moon is in whose house. Leave that to the hard-core and the faintly loony—the people with charts. What you want to do here is either dismiss the whole thing (i.e., When asked what your sign is, answer, "The best") or make a bit of sense, if humanly possible. Here are the proper clichés, sign by sign:

Aquarius (January 20–February 18) Creative and modern-thinking. Often mistaken for not too bright. Does not learn from experience.

Pisces (February 19–March 20) Emotionally powerful, if a bit paranoid. Makes up for a lack of real bravery by being a bully. Has no pets.

Aries (March 21–April 19) Outdoorsy and independent. Walks away rather than has a decent discussion.

Taurus (April 20–May 20) Great stick-with-it-ness. Often wealthy later in life, usually through crooked means.

Gemini (May 21–June 20) Intelligent, if schizophrenic. Neither aspect of personality admirable. Fast at making deals, fast at losing friends.

Cancer (June 21–July 22) A good listener, easy to take advantage of. Wildly emotional, barely able to function in adult environment.

Leo (July 23–August 22) Stubborn and forceful. Seems to listen but doesn't really care. Makes a good cop.

Virgo (August 23–September 22) Weighs facts carefully, often resulting in complete inaction. Obsessively clean and hard to be with because of it.

Libra (September 23–October 22) Sensitive to music, art, and literature. Happy completely alone, making everyone grateful for it.

Scorpio (October 23–November 21) One-way sensitivity. Easily hurt, but unconscious of others' feelings. Makes excellent file clerk.

Sagittarius (November 22–December 21) Loves to gamble, often loses. Sees the bright side of everything, however senseless.

Capricorn (December 22–January 19) Tends to be private and as a result, learns little. Is best as a child.

If all else fails, when pushed by patchouli-wearing, pentagram-dangling obsessive, just say "I don't believe in astrology. I realize that's very Leo of me, but what can I say?"

CHAPTER TWENTY-ONE:

PSYCHIATRY/PSYCHOLOGY

HEAD TRIPS AND TRICKS

The evening is shaping up. You're with a fresh group of people—maybe your new coworkers, or perhaps your latest significant other's college pals. It's going great: easy talk, they get your jokes, there's none of that "what else do we have in common" awkwardness. There's no reason not to think that these people could eventually become part of your "tribe."

Until . . .

Chances are it's only a stray word, or an insignificant gesture that triggers the beginning of a conversational black hole. But once under way, there's not a chance of throwing the talk back into—oh, let's be honest—interesting territory.

"Have you discussed that with your therapist?" you hear the girl with cute glasses ask her floppy-banged friend. "Oh yeah. We've been

working on it for a while." "Hmmm . . . Have you thought about bodywork?"

Of course, the preceding exchange can come across in any one of a zillion variations—replace "bodywork" for "reiki," "Ritalin," or "gluten-free diet." The problem is, you can't help but wonder if Glasses is playing a trick on Floppy Bangs. The last time you checked, bodywork was an icky synonym for "happy ending massage." Or could you be wrong? Maybe stretching does cure psychic trauma? Just because you took a Freud class in college doesn't mean you know everything about psychology, even if you got an A. These ladies could just be clued in to something you don't get—wheat berries will make you bipolar!—and if you don't act as if you know what they do, they're going to lecture you on neural pathways in the brain until you need a double dose of Wellbutrin just to catch a cab home.

Like it or not, we live in an age where acting as if you have a degree from the Mayo Clinic's psych program (are they even a school?) is *de rigueur* among a certain over-educated, under-employed demographic. Furthermore, any suggestion that you have been going, day by day, sorting out your issues without a staff of thousands . . . Well, it's just nothing that you want to have to fess up to, especially once everyone in the crowd has touted their latest energetic healing breakthrough.

"So does your insurance cover that?" you ask, as Glasses emphatically shakes her head. "This is an investment in myself." Oh, right. But aren't new shoes a lot more fun? And, ultimately, except stilettos, much more practical? It's an understandable argument, but unfortunately, it's also so unhip, so ignorant, so totally close-minded that your best bet is to forget it before you even begin it.

Psycho-anything—*therapy, somatic, neurotic, analysis*—is just another way of writing $$$$$, which of course is part of its charm. To have healers in various disciplines confirms you as a big spender. It's right up there with having the big Louis Vuitton bag or a standing winter trip to St. Barts.

It further suggests that you're a person for whom time, that unpleasant worry of the working class, means nothing, because who could get their chakras and spine into alignment in a couple of $1.98 quickie sessions? Okay, fine—most of the population of India, who manage to do such things while living in poverty, but let's not split hairs.

So, if you've had no personal experience with strict Freudian analysis, color therapy, Alexander Technique, or otherwise, it's obvious that you are going to have to fake it.

Don't be nervous. Just a few stock phrases will get you launched. Fortunately, unlike in stock car racing, hedge fund founding, or real estate, feelings take precedent over facts, and generalities outrank specifics.

You establish your credentials with something simple:

"Don't you find the search for bliss excessively solipsistic?"

"Bettelheim's theories about childhood personality formation were discredited years ago."

"I guess I have trouble relating to the idea that aromatic oils are just as effective for depression as good, old fashioned talk therapy."

Once the ball starts rolling, you'll find your input can be minimal provided it's punctuated by one of a dozen or so phrases including the following: serotonin deficit; overcoming post-traumatic stress disorder; learning to love my parents, finally; our therapeutic process; my inner child needs . . .

If pressed for clarification of anything, you can either freewheel it, or if sensing yourself on thin ice, you can take refuge in a murmured suggestion that until you've worked your way through a difficult impasse, you'd prefer not to explore the subject in any greater depth. In contrast to, say, tennis or checkers, the act of retreating in the face of a discussion about your own emotional path will win you the respectful understanding of your audience. Retreat therefore should be considered a legitimate option.

The whole world of psychology, psychiatry, and emotional healing is more splintered than a seaside boardwalk. If you should happen to stumble across someone who seems to have secured even a tentative grip on any one particular school of thought, you have only to veer smoothly off in another direction, confident that no good Rolfian is going to be able to chase after a kundalini devotee (they know breathing as well as any marathoner); few psychopharm patients will have the patience for acupuncture; and no analysand will be able to take a starry-eyed new ager seriously.

And God forbid you should even discuss the idea of long-term therapy anywhere except for a major city. Most Americans a) don't have health insurance that will cover more than a few headshrinking sessions per decade, and b) think talking about your problems—let alone attacking—is so much unpatriotic navel gazing. Therefore, if you want to sound like an expert outside of Chicago, L.A., or New York, do yourself a favor and explain that Lindsay Lohan has just started this new primal scream therapy in her latest rehab, but you did it five years ago, when she was still acting in Disney movies. If, however, you have the misfortune to get yourself into a conversation with someone who seems to have some honest-to-God firsthand knowledge of the subject, you should, without hesitation, cut off your previous remarks abruptly. Then, squeeze out some tears (this goes over especially well if you're a guy), and whisper:

"Wow, I really thought I could talk about all this stuff now . . . Nope, still too painful."

"All I can say is, I know how to cry now, and that is no thanks to my parents."

"There are so many ways growing up in a cult requires you to remake yourself once you leave . . ."

All of these comments will leave your listeners so simultaneously fascinated, frightened, and repelled that they won't know whether to ask you more questions, buy you dinner, or run screaming. And that sort of confusion is very good for a faker's social life. Keep's 'em in the stalls, as Barnum used to say (see Chapter 103 for faking knowledge of historic hucksters—made you look!).

Some key phrases for continuing the conversation:

> "Didn't Freud prove to us once and for all that the origins of our sexual proclivities are not to be found in our conscious choices? Hmmm?"
>
> "Wow, I am really amazed that in the twenty-first century some people still don't believe in the idea of repressed-memory syndrome."

Finally, do please remember that in this league the most demeaning thing you can be called—the lowest status to which you can be reduced—is normal.

CHAPTER TWENTY TWO:

SOCIALIZING

CASUAL AND PROFESSIONAL

Even more than elsewhere in this book, this section relies on attitude. Elsewhere you have facts to back you up and one-up your companions; here you've got to think on your feet. The situations described here are, if not quite life-saving, at least career- and face-saving.

We're referring to those awkward situations we find ourselves in on a daily basis either professionally or socially. Some might call the advice you're about to get a "liar's manual"; we prefer to see it as a way to avoid hurting someone else's feelings while appearing to be both good and wise.

Situation: You're at the mall and you bump into an old college acquaintance and his or her spouse. They're strolling a baby carriage, coming right at you. Your feelings about seeing them don't matter, nor do theirs toward you. The baby's the thing. It's asleep, and you're invited to peek into the pram. What you see is something out of Wes Craven by way of John Carpenter—quite simply, an ugly baby. Most of them are, of course—little Winston Churchills and Dwight Eisenhowers—but not in their parents' eyes. Only an infant's parents can actually tell the difference between their child and someone else's or notice features, smiles, and eye color; what you see is a blob of flesh that looks like a clenched fist. Here are some things you can say and still remain on speaking terms with the progenitors of this little darling:

> "Mmm, that's some baby!"
>
> "How old is (s)he? (S)he's so big/tiny!"
>
> "Just look at those hands." (Not to use if something is wrong with baby's hands—always check for webbing or the like first.)
>
> "Wow!? (S)he's a perfect combination of the two of you." (Not to be used in case of adoption or a single parent situation.)

These may just seem like common sense, but when faced with something amazingly irregular, you never know what you may blurt out. And "My! She has such a beautiful eye!" or "I had no idea that hair could grow from there" simply won't do. Neither will "Oh my God, what happened?" Keep your cool and have your line at the ready.

Situation: You've just bumped into someone whose phone calls and/or e-mails you've been avoiding for weeks. Here is where technology becomes your friend. Pre-empt with:

> "I've been trying to reach you for weeks. Is your machine broken?"
>
> "Thank God you're OK—someone told me you left your job and the two e-mails I sent last week bounced back."
>
> "How great to see you—my cell was stolen, and it had all my numbers in it." Or alternately, "Glad I ran into you—that new Dell laptop crashed and ate my whole address and phone book."

Should you be dealing with a Luddite, with no e-mail or answering machine, try "Oh, forgive me for not getting back to you, but you must have heard about the terrible fire and my old friend Billy . . ." (voice trails off here in semi-despair).

If you accidentally pick up the phone and it's someone you don't want to talk to, you can start screaming, "You're breaking up—I can't hear you" and hang up after making clicking or boom-box noises while you're talking. Alternatively, tell the person you'll call them right back. Call them immediately and then complain about a bad connection, click and grind, and disconnect. For the latter, you get points for trying, too.

Situation: You bump into your boss or someone you've been trying to impress and you've had a handful of drinks too many.

> "I'm fine except for this cold—and these anthistamines are knocking me out. Excuse me before I infect everyone."

Situation: Discussion turns to a news story you really should know about and you are totally uninformed.

> Laugh and say, "What do you think "The Daily Show" will do with that one?"

Situation: You are invited to see an artistic friend perform, and it is beyond awful.

> "You couldn't have been any better," or "You must have wanted to be a performer in the worst way," or "You should have been in the audience," or just shake your head, smile and say, "You, you, you."

At the end of any of these encounters, look a your watch, say, "Holy shit!," excuse yourself, and make a quick exit.